values
IN
evaluation
AND
social
research

values
IN
evaluation
AND
social
research

Ernest R. House
Kenneth R. Howe

Sage Publications
International Educational and Professional Publisher
Thousand Oaks   London   New Delhi

For information:

Sage Publications, Inc.
2455 Teller Road
Thousand Oaks, California 91320
E-mail: order@sagepub.com

Sage Publications Ltd.
6 Bonhill Street
London EC2A 4PU
United Kingdom

Sage Publications India Pvt. Ltd.
M-32 Market
Greater Kailash I
New Delhi 110 048 India

Printed in the United States of America

Library of Congress Cataloging-in-Publication Data

House, Ernest R.
    Values in evaluation and social research / by Ernest R. House
and Kenneth R. Howe.
        p.   cm.
    ISBN 0-7619-1154-5 (cloth: alk. paper)
    ISBN 0-7619-1155-3 (pbk.: alk. paper)
    1. Evaluation research (Social action programs)   2. Social
sciences—Research.   I. Howe, Kenneth Ross.   II. Title.
H62 .H645   1999
300′.7′2—dc21   99-6434

This book is printed on acid-free paper.

01   02   03   04   05   7   6   5   4   3   2

Acquiring Editor:	C. Deborah Laughton
Editorial Assistant:	Eileen Carr
Production Editor:	Denise Santoyo
Editorial Assistant:	Patricia Zeman
Designer/Typesetter:	Lynn Miyata
Cover Designer:	Kathy White

For Georgia,
Is that all there is?
and
In loving memory of Jean

CONTENTS

————•◆•————

Part III. Deliberative Democratic Evaluation

PREFACE

————•◆•————

Our aspiration in this book is to reconcile evaluation theory with general currents in contemporary philosophy. Although evaluators regularly borrow ideas from philosophers, many important insights of the past 20 years of philosophy remain untapped. Hence, we, an evaluator and a philosopher, have taken on this joint task. The task is not simply one of converting concepts from one field to the other. The discourse styles of the two fields differ significantly, and even though we have tried to smooth out these differences, the reader may experience occasional jolts as we switch from one discourse to the other. Philosophical discourse tends to be denser, tougher, and, yes, more irritating than that in evaluation. This is Socrates' legacy. We apologize in advance to those who may take offense at this more aggressive style of analysis. Those who read philosophy will be used to it.

To accomplish this task, we focus on the infamous fact-value dichotomy, an unresolved issue central to evaluation. We see how this issue is addressed in philosophy currently and apply these insights to evaluation theory, as well as add our own original analysis to the topic. This is not to suggest that philosophy has all the answers, by any means. Indeed, the limits of philosophy have been made clearer as we have developed this book. However, philosophers have carefully considered many relevant issues, and combining ideas from the two different fields yields insights not available otherwise.

The focus of this book is on evaluation theory rather than on practice, even though we do suggest implications for practice. We believe theory is used to justify and inform practice, so the theory makes a difference to practice over the long run. And practice can inform theory, as it has done many times in the past. But, again, our focus is on reconciling evaluation theory with philosophy, which means this is not a how-to-do-it book. Rather, it is a book that develops middle-range evaluation theory consistent with contemporary thinking in philosophy (albeit a particular strand), especially thinking about democracy. A middle-range theory would suggest some attributes that evaluations should have, without necessarily specifying how to achieve them in particular cases. So the book offers a perspective about evaluation rather than a model of how to do evaluation.

Many people now practicing evaluation already do much of what we recommend, for reasons not having to do with formal philosophy, relying on their own experience and intuition. We deliberately tie our theoretical conclusions to practices already existing, where we can, to give credit to those who have practiced these ideas in advance of our analysis and to demonstrate that such studies can be done.

Although our attention is centered on evaluation, we believe these insights apply to educational and social research as well, because they are haunted by similar value issues. Evaluation and social research often blend together, but they can be distinguished from each other. Evaluation arrives at conclusions such as "X is good," whereas social research arrives at conclusions such as "X causes Y" or "X is a case of Y." Where Y can be demonstrated as something worthwhile, the two are similar.

In both evaluation and social research, investigators face similar value issues and cannot be value-neutral, in our view. Rather, investigators in both fields can arrive at objective, impartial value judgments. However, providing examples of how our analysis applies to educational and social research would have required a longer and more complicated book. So we have focused on evaluation alone.

ACKNOWLEDGMENTS

Some of the ideas discussed in this book have appeared previously in Ernest R. House, "The Problem of Values in Evaluation," *Evaluation Journal of Australasia* (1997); in Ernest R. House and Kenneth R. Howe, "Advocacy in Evaluation," *American Journal of Evaluation* (1998); in Kenneth R. Howe, "Democracy, Justice and Action Research: Some Theoretical Developments," *Educational Action Research* (1995); and in Kenneth R. Howe, "The Interpretive Turn and the New Debate in Education," *Educational Researcher* (1998).

We especially wish to acknowledge the assistance of Ove Karlsson and the reviewers of the manuscript—Robert E. Stake, University of Illinois at Urbana-Champaign, Michael Morris, University of New Haven, Gary T. Henry, Georgia State University, and Michael Quinn Patton, author of *Utilization-Focused Evaluation*—for invaluable advice on revisions, which have been extensive. Thanks also go to C. Deborah Laughton for her patience and skill in working through the stylistic and conceptual difficulties.

INTRODUCTION

The Problem of Values

———•◆•———

valuators are confronted with many pieces of professional advice that often conflict with one another. Here are some examples:

❑ Evaluators should be value-neutral.

❑ Evaluators should be advocates for certain groups.

❑ Evaluators should treat all stakeholder views as equally worthy.

❑ Evaluators should weigh and balance stakeholder views.

❑ Evaluators should admit all stakeholder views as legitimate.

❑ Evaluators should take the views of the sponsors of the study.

❑ Evaluators should engage in dialogue with stakeholders.

❑ Evaluators should remain aloof from stakeholders.

❑ Evaluators should act only as facilitators.

❑ Evaluators should draw conclusions in their studies.

❏ Evaluators should not draw conclusions.

❏ Evaluators should draw partial conclusions.

❏ Values determine methodology.

❏ Values have nothing to do with methodology.

❏ Values are subjective.

❏ Values are objective.

These opinions derive from different conceptions of evaluation, based on different assumptions. In fact, some of the most hotly contested disputes in evaluation revolve around these so-called value issues. These are issues evaluators get excited about, even though the issues are complex indeed, rooted in the ways we think about the world. We believe that most of these different beliefs stem from disagreements about the nature of facts and values at a fundamental level. In one view facts and values are dichotomous. Even though evaluators can legitimately determine facts, they cannot do so with values, in this view. Values are simply chosen by people and are not subject to rational determination. Hence, evaluators must draw conclusions based on stakeholder and client values without critiquing those values. Or they must strongly qualify the conclusions of studies to correspond to client or stakeholder values.

A counter view is that not only do people choose their values, they also choose their own facts—a radical constructivist view. In this view, facts are like values in that it is a matter of individual choice as to the facts we choose to believe and the weight we give to them in our reasoning. In a sense, individuals construct their own worlds, their own realities. Hence, evaluators should assume the role of neutral facilitators in how they handle the facts and values of other people. In this view, expertise has no special role to play. People must decide for themselves. All is relative to the individual's view.

We don't think either of these two widespread views provides the proper basis for evaluation. We want to cast the core fact-value distinction another way. We want to contend that fact and value statements are not dichotomous; rather, the two blend together. Evaluative statements consist of fact and value claims intertwined, melded together, and so do most claims in evaluation.

Furthermore, we contend that evaluators can draw objective value conclusions by collecting and analyzing evidence and following the procedures of their professional discipline. Such a view legitimates professional activities and opens the way to a stronger social role for evaluation. It provides evaluation with more authority in public decision making, a much-needed service in contemporary society, in our view.

In order to perform these tasks, evaluators need some conception of their role that is compatible with democracy. Indeed, we think that those who are active in evaluation must have some broad conception of how their studies will be used in democratic societies, even if these views are implicit. Our aim is to align theory and professional practice with democratic thinking. This is not a utopian goal; from our point of view, many evaluators already engage in good practices. In this book we explicate the theoretical justification behind such practices, consistent with contemporary thinking about democracy, and develop a conception of how such practices can contribute to democracy.

THE ARGUMENT OF THIS BOOK

The first part of the book deals with the nature of values and value claims. The status of value judgments has long been a contentious issue, and the dispute has carried over into evaluation, significantly impeding the development of the field. One legacy of positivism in the 20th century has been that facts and values are viewed as entirely distinct. Facts have to do with the real world and values with the worth humans place on factual situations. Hence, values are inherently subjective, and value judgments have no cognitive foundation. This means that evaluators cannot legitimately make value judgments. Those judgments must be arrived at by other means, such as by letting the audiences of the evaluation decide.

In our analysis, fact and value statements exist on a continuum, where they blend into one another (Chapter 1). Even though certain facts and values occupy the extreme ends of the continuum, many such statements blend together in the center of the continuum and possess both fact and value dimensions that cannot be fully distinguished from each other. This is especially true of evaluative statements and the concepts from social research that evaluators often employ. The concept of IQ is a good example: It has both factual and value aspects to it.

In our view, evaluators can arrive at valid evaluative conclusions if they follow the proper rules and procedures of their discipline. This does not mean that evaluators should make decisions for policy makers or clients, only that constrained evaluative judgments, properly arrived at, can provide input into such decisions, which also include considerations other than the findings of professional evaluation (Chapter 2).

As explicated by Scriven (1980), the logic of evaluation consists of finding criteria for the evaluation, setting performance standards for each criterion, collecting relevant data, and summing the data and criteria into overall judgments of success or failure of the policies, programs, products, or whatever is under review. Of course, this formal logic does not capture the full complexity of evaluative reasoning any more than syllogisms capture the full complexity of human reasoning (Stake et al., 1997).

The actual evaluative process is more complex and is dependent on many substantive and contextual considerations as well as the nature of the entity being evaluated. The context of the evaluation is critical in limiting the logical possibilities of evaluations and making solutions possible. Evaluators do not have to consider all criteria or all potential audiences, only those relevant to a particular time and place in a particular context. Although evaluators differ as to how agreement on criteria is obtained, who participates in the evaluation process, and how performance criteria and data are handled, they can nonetheless arrive at reasonable levels of agreement using the concepts and tools of their discipline.

CRITIQUES OF OTHER VIEWS

The second part of the book critiques three prominent views. The first is the "received view" of facts and values (Chapter 3). The received view has dominated evaluation since the 1960s. Perhaps the clearest expression of the received view is found in the work of Donald Campbell (1982). Although Campbell rejects positivist epistemology, he advocates maintaining the fact-value distinction as a way to preserve objective, bias-free social research. Similarly, Shadish, Cook, and Leviton (1995) distinguish between descriptive and prescriptive valuing and contend that ultimate value judgments apply only to those who hold them.

The received view places some value constraints on evaluation, but these constraints are minimal. The received view takes at least two forms: means depiction and interest group depiction. Means depiction embraces some goal, such as academic achievement or minimizing cost, and investigates the means of attaining that goal, the best means to the given end. Interest group depiction allows values and interests from different groups to be considered and contends that both are worthy of equal consideration. It results in statements such as "X is good from the perspective of stakeholder group Y."

These approaches are inadequate from our point of view. Means depiction makes no provision for the participation of other affected parties, and interest group depiction makes no provision for the imbalance of power among groups or for the differential moral force that might attach to the claims of different groups. Hence, "value minimalists" confront a dilemma: They either exclude the values of other groups or possibly produce value anarchy once values are admitted.

The interpretive turn in evaluation provides the justification for including insider perspectives and the "voices" of those who have been marginalized or excluded (Chapter 4). As opposed to a "spectator view" of knowledge, in which knowledge is built up piece by piece by accumulation and passive observation, interpretivists share a "constructivist view." In this view, knowledge is actively constructed through interaction and dialogue, which means that it is culturally and historically grounded and laden with moral and political values, which often serve particular interests.

The resulting dialogical approaches embrace the melding of facts and values in evaluation, denying that such melding can be avoided. Although we accept a version of the dialogical position in working out the deliberative democratic view, we question two other versions: radical constructivism and postmodernism. Radical constructivism takes at face value the reports of stakeholders as to what is happening because they have privileged positions as insiders (e.g., Guba & Lincoln, 1989).

Values are automatically included via dialogical interaction—a good thing. However, radical constructivists do not go beyond stakeholder neutrality. Outsider perspectives cannot be admitted in this approach, at least not authoritatively. Hence, evaluators must defer to stakeholders regarding the effects of social programs and policies, limiting the evaluators' role to facilitation. The problem is that insiders may well be wrong or biased in their interpretations, a bias potentially countered by the inclusion of outsider perspectives.

Postmodernism is more difficult to characterize, but it rejects the idea that the views of insiders are unproblematic (Chapter 5). Indeed, postmodernists see social life as shrouded in contingencies that must be problematized, deconstructed, and disrupted. In postmodernism, investigators must question the taken-for-granted but ungrounded social norms and practices that oppress people. For example, evaluators might send deliberately irritating questionnaires to respondents to incite them to question the authority of the evaluation itself and what it represents (e.g., Stronach & MacLure, 1997).

Postmodernists also refuse to render value conclusions and are suspicious of those who do. Public knowledge and professional expertise are seen as oppressive in general. Hence, postmodernists are in the contradictory position of undermining any value judgments whatsoever, including their own. It is difficult to see how a practical activity such as evaluation, which seeks to offer public guidance, could confine itself to nothing but disruption and deconstruction.

THE DELIBERATIVE DEMOCRATIC VIEW

The third part of this book deals with the deliberative democratic view, our preferred view. The deliberative democratic view rejects value minimalism and relativism (Chapter 6). Unlike the means depiction approaches, it does not assume one goal and try to maximize it. Unlike other received view approaches, it does not embrace mere interest group depiction. It is dialogical but, unlike radical constructivism, it does not assume that insiders are always correct. Unlike postmodernism, it employs public criteria to evaluate and contribute to public knowledge.

The deliberative democratic view is explicitly committed to the values of democracy, to the conduct of evaluation from an explicit democratic framework, and to the responsibility of evaluators to uphold these values. The aim is for evaluators to use procedures that incorporate the views of insiders and outsiders, give voice to the marginal and excluded, employ reasoned criteria in extended deliberation, and engage in dialogical interactions with significant audiences and stakeholders in the evaluation.

It is patently obvious that stakeholder groups in fact do not have equal power and that dialogue among them is not fully democratic in the sense of being undistorted by power relationships, hidden or overt. Evaluators should strive to remedy this problem by ensuring that free and unobstructed deliberations are carried out in the conduct of the evaluation, in planning, design, and interpretation. Evaluators should not assume that all group opinions are equally correct. In fact, some stakeholder views may be ruled out on democratic grounds.

Evaluations should meet three explicit requirements: inclusion, dialogue, and deliberation. First, evaluations should include all major stakeholder interests and views in some form. Second, they should allow for extensive dialogue so that stakeholder views and interests are authentic, as represented in the evaluation. Third, they should provide for sufficient deliberation so that valid conclusions can be arrived at, deliberation that utilizes the expertise of evaluators. When the evaluation meets such requirements, as well as those typically associated with proper data collection and analysis, we call the study democratic, impartial, and objective.

Of course, evaluators must conduct their work in concrete social conditions, and proponents of the deliberative democratic view must recognize that it is too idealized to be straightforwardly implemented in the world of policy and practice (Chapter 7). An uncompromising commitment to the deliberative democratic view, in which evaluators make no compromises and accept nothing short of the ideal, would be "impractical." But we should avoid making the best the enemy of the better. It does not follow that because the ideal of deliberative democracy cannot be fully attained under present conditions, it should not be approximated.

Evaluators should not ignore imbalances of power or pretend that dialogue about evaluation is open when it is not. To do so is to endorse status quo power arrangements implicitly. We believe that the best solution is for evaluators to face the power issues squarely and adopt a position of democratic deliberation as the ideal for the adjudication of public value claims. In this conception evaluators are neither bystanders nor philosopher kings. In Chapter 7 we examine the work of several evaluators who have attempted to establish such democratic dialogues.

Finally, we conclude this volume with a discussion of the role of evaluation in democratic, advanced capitalist societies. These are societies with formidable institutions of advertising, public relations,

and mass media. Claims and counterclaims are rampant. Such societies need cognitive institutions like evaluation that serve to discern
true from false assertions and determine the worth of products,
programs, policies, and performance. Such institutions support
democratic decision making by providing sound knowledge on which
to base decisions.

In this sense, evaluation serves the needs of a deliberative democracy, not an "emotivist" one. In an emotivist (or preferential) democracy,
the views or values of citizens are taken as given. Values are not
subject to deliberation as to their worth. By contrast, in a deliberative
democracy, the views, preferences, and values of all citizens are
subject to deliberation and debate as to their worthiness.

The deliberative democratic view applies to evaluation generally
as an institution as well as to individual studies. It interweaves an
egalitarian conception of justice that seeks to equalize power in arriving at evaluative conclusions with the three general requirements—
inclusion, dialogue, and deliberation.

In our view, evaluators have a fiduciary responsibility to participants in evaluations and to the public to use their expertise to further
the public interest. Sometimes they must be savvy negotiators, willing to engage in compromise, but they must also place limits on how
far compromise can go and be uncompromising about morally objectionable claims. Evaluators must take stands on the requirements of
democracy.

PART I

Value Claims

1

FACTS AND VALUES

————•◆•————

n the first undergraduate philosophy course, starting
with the pre-Socratic philosophers, instructors often
introduce students to Zeno's paradox, one form of
which is that if you try to leave the room, at some point in time you
will be halfway to the door. An instant later you will be half that
distance, then half that distance again, and half again, on to infinity.
In other words, by traversing half the distance each time, regardless
of the time elapsed, logically you can never leave the room.

Obviously, something is wrong with this reasoning, because you
can actually leave the room. Leaving the room is not properly modeled
by the implicit infinite mathematical progression that the paradox
assumes. The model is inappropriate for the task at hand—getting
out of the room. This is the kind of difficulty that clever philosophers
sometimes manufacture by the way they cast problems, even when
the results of their analyses contradict common sense.

The "value-free" doctrine of social research is reminiscent of Zeno's paradox, except that the value-free doctrine has had more pernicious effects than Zeno's paradox ever did. There are not many people sitting around in rooms saying they can't get out, but there are large numbers of people, including professional evaluators, saying they cannot make value judgments, or that they can, but doing so is illicit. The value-free doctrine, in conjunction with an inadequate notion of causation, has seriously impeded the progress of social research (House, 1990). This doctrine says that we cannot make value judgments rationally and legitimately, just as Zeno's paradox tells us we can't walk out the door. In fact, we do both all the time.

Skepticism toward values has existed in various guises since Plato's time, and perhaps before. In Plato's *Republic*, the Sophist Thrasymachus scoffs at Socrates' attempt to employ reason to understand justice. Justice is "what's in the interest of the stronger," Thrasymachus proclaims. Modern skepticism toward values can be traced back to Hobbes and Hume, the latter of whom states the issue in this form:

> Reason is, and ought only to be the slave of the passions, and can never pretend to any other office than to serve and obey them. . . . Since morals . . . have an influence on the actions and affections, it follows, that they cannot be deriv'd from reason; and that because reason alone . . . can never have any such influence. Morals excite passions, and produce or prevent actions. Reason of itself is utterly impotent in this particular. The rules of morality, therefore, are not conclusions of our reason. (Hume, 1739/1978, pp. 415, 457)

> 'Tis not contrary to reason to prefer the destruction of the whole world to the scratching of my finger. 'Tis not contrary to reason for me to chuse my total ruin, to prevent the least uneasiness of an Indian or person wholly unknown to me. 'Tis as little contrary to reason to prefer even my own ac-

knowledged lesser good to my greater, and have a more ardent affection for the former than the latter. (Hume, 1739/1978, p. 416)

Hume's view is echoed by influential 20th-century philosophers (e.g., the positivists) and social scientists (e.g., the Weberians). From these perspectives, value claims are (merely) expressions of feelings or attitudes of approval or assertions of will. They exemplify moral subjectivism, the belief that moral positions are not grounded in reason or in the nature of things; rather, we simply adopt them because we are drawn to them emotionally. Ultimately, value claims are matters of choice not grounded in rationality, and, as such, are outside the realm of scientific investigation.

A central tenet of our argument in this book is that value claims can be based on reason, properly understood, and that they can be objective in a straightforward sense of that word. We contend that evaluation incorporates value judgments (even if implicitly) both in its methodological frameworks and in the concepts employed, concepts such as "intelligence" or "community" or "disadvantaged." We also argue that these value commitments should be explicated and examined if evaluation is to be morally and politically self-reflective. Evaluators can arrive at value claims legitimately as part of their professional duties if they follow the principles, rules, and procedures of their profession. They also should be prepared to defend such value claims.

THE FACT-VALUE CONTINUUM

Admittedly, "value" is not the most precise concept. As Frankena (1967) has noted, "The terms 'value' and 'valuation' and their cognates and compounds are used in a confused and confusing but widespread way in our contemporary culture, not only in economics and philosophy, but also and especially in other social sciences and humanities" (p. 229). At one time the meaning was reasonably clear.

Value meant the worth of a thing, and *valuation* meant an estimate of its worth. This is the primary conception of value that we employ: An evaluation is the determination of the worth, merit, or "value" of something, particularly in the professional evaluation of products, programs, policies, and performance (Scriven, 1991). In this sense, professional evaluation requires deliberation and is not based on unreflective cherishing or desiring.

However, we cannot escape other uses of the term entirely. *Value* is used broadly as a concrete noun to refer to what has value or is thought to be good—for example, *democratic values, conservative values,* or *stakeholder values.* Often behind this conception of value is the covert assumption that nothing really has objective value; rather, a thing has value only because it is regarded as having value or is thought to be valuable—back to the subjective notion again that values are detached from reasonable assessment and depend on individual choice somehow.

This meaning of value is common in the evaluation and social research communities. Hence, we hear how stakeholder "values" (things stakeholders believe to be important) are used in an evaluation study. The term *values* used in this broad way may refer to opinions, beliefs, preferences, interests, wants, needs, or desires. Usually it is not defined in any precise way. When we use the term *value* in this book, we will try to be clear about which meaning we intend. Sometimes we refer to value conclusions rationally determined and sometimes to preferences, beliefs, interests, and so on that are not subject to strong evidential support.

In fact, we should specify the way we conceive the fact-value dichotomy generally. According to Hume, facts and values have separate referents, which can mean either that values do not mingle with facts or that values cannot be derived from facts. In both cases values are detached from facts altogether. By contrast, our view is that fact and value statements merge together on a continuum, something like this (House, 1997):

Brute Facts ———————————————————— Bare Values

To the left of the continuum are statements such as "Diamonds are harder than steel," which have nothing to do with personal taste. To the right of the continuum are statements such as "Cabernet sauvignon is better than chardonnay," which have much to do with personal taste. In the center are statements such as "A is more intelligent than B," "This test is valid," and "X is a good program." These statements are neither brute facts nor bare values; they blend facts and values together. The statements can be right or wrong and also have strong value implications.

Whether a claim counts as a brute fact or bare value or something in between depends partly on context. For example, "John Doe is dead" used to look much like a brute fact without much of a value implication. Yet what if John Doe is hooked up to a life-support system that is maintaining his breathing and heartbeat, but he is in an irreversible coma? The contemporary judgment that he is dead requires a shift in the meaning of the concept, one spurred by judgments of value, such as what constitutes good "quality of life." What was once pretty much a brute fact has become considerably value-laden because of medical technology.

Professional evaluative statements fall toward the center of the fact-value continuum for the most part. They are statements derived from a particular institution, the evolving institution of evaluation. Whether a statement is true and objective is determined by the procedures established by professional evaluators according to the rules and concepts of their profession. Some human judgments are involved, constructed according to criteria of the institution, but their human origin does not necessarily make them objectively untrue.

Consider Stake's (1995) opening words in his evaluation of Harper School:

Chicago School Reform was a major focus of attention among educators everywhere. But not in Chicago's Harper Elementary School. Attention there was on the challenging, burdensome, discouraging work of day-to-day teaching and running the school. To the staff, systemwide school reform was an abstraction, more than a little far removed from reality.

Harper's School Improvement Plan (SIP) called for improvement in reading, multicultural studies, preparation for further education, even getting the leaky windows repaired. But what consumed the energy of the pedagogical day was even more mundane: accounting for the absent and tardy; finding but one student completing the homework assignment; confronting indomitable rebels; restraining lunchtime lines, one to the cafeteria, one to the exit, until other classes cleared. (p. 137)

Stake spends the first several pages of his study describing his visit to the school, the school's appearance, meeting the principal, and so on. By the time readers have finished the description of the school, even the first paragraphs, they are well informed as to what Stake thinks about Chicago school reform generally. He artfully weaves his evaluation conclusions into the descriptive introduction. Is this description? Yes. Is it evaluation? Yes. The context often determines whether statements are evaluative, and statements can be descriptive and evaluative at the same time. The study also is objective in the sense that Stake can be right or wrong about Chicago school reform. His observations can be incorrect, or he may draw the wrong conclusions.

Evaluative statements can be objective in the sense that we can present evidence for their truth or falsity, just as for other statements. In these statements factual and value aspects blend together. For example, a statement such as "Social welfare increases helplessness" has value built in. It requires an understanding of social welfare and helplessness, and these concepts are heavily value-laden. Is the statement true? We decide its truth within the evidential procedures of evaluation. We present evidence and make arguments that are recognized and accepted within the discipline. There are disciplinary frameworks for making such judgments objectively.

So objectivity in our sense means that a statement can be true or false, that it is objective if it is unbiased (Scriven, 1972), that evidence can be collected for or against the statement's truth or falsity, and that procedures defined by the discipline provide rules for the handling of such evidence so that it is unbiased. Scriven (1991) in particular has championed the idea of objective value claims. Of course, if someone wants to take the skeptical view that any human judgment or concept of any kind is subjective, then all these statements are subjective. But then so is the statement "Diamonds are harder than steel," which depends on concepts of diamonds and steel, even though the referents are physical entities.

The sense of objectivity we wish to reject explicitly is the positivist notion that objectivity depends on stripping away all conceptual and value aspects and getting down to the bedrock of pristine facts. Rather, being objective in our sense means working toward unbiased statements through the procedures of the discipline, observing the canons of proper argument and methodology, maintaining a healthy skepticism, and being vigilant to eradicate sources of bias. We deny that it is the evaluator's job to determine only the factual claims and leave the value claims to someone else, as some do. Evaluators can determine value claims too. Indeed, they can hardly avoid doing so.

VALUES AS EMERGENT

The continuum we have suggested is one of fact-value statements after the speaker has arrived at some conclusion. Having stated value claims makes the matter seem settled, as if it were that way all the time. However, the construction of value claims may be emergent. To illustrate, suppose someone were to ask the following: "What do you think of changing the U.S. political system to a parliamentary one, on the model of Israel's?"

We might say something along the following lines: "Well, we can see real advantages to a system in which minority views can be heard, even if they don't win out, in preference to our system, in which all we hear are the views of those who have captured a majority of votes by patching together watered-down, least-controversial policies. But we really need more information. We're not that familiar with the Israeli system, and we assume that we would want to modify it to fit our situation as well."

Based on this exchange, would it be correct to say we "value" moving to the Israeli system? Probably not. But it would not be quite accurate to say we don't value it either. After further interaction in which we could get key questions answered, we might well come down on one side or the other. And we would be able to make a statement about the Israeli system that includes our reasoning about it.

Many issues about "who values what" are like this. In this example, suppose, after further interaction in which the information we want is provided, we wind up supporting a move to a parliamentary system. Was this value there all along or is it newly constructed? It's hard to say. In one sense it was *there* all along, but could be uncovered only through dialogue and reflection. In another sense it was not *there* but has been constructed, given that we couldn't articulate a position at the outset. But why worry about this question anyway?

Our view is that evaluators should be concerned with what people believe *upon reflection*. This is the most important sense of what people *really* believe vis-à-vis social policy and program initiatives. This emergence of value claims through deliberation, accomplished partly through dialogue, is what a robust democracy requires—or so we will contend. Values (value claims) can be merely unexamined preferences, but good evaluations are well considered by all relevant parties. We would like to see such deliberation built into evaluation. The question then becomes, What are the conditions that produce well-considered value claims? We turn to the concept of democracy itself for answers to what constitutes proper deliberation when the claims of many stakeholders conflict.

VALUES AND DEMOCRATIC DELIBERATION

It seems to us that evaluators anticipate the social conditions in which their findings will be received, in at least a vague way. Further, they conceive these conditions as being "democratic" in most instances because most evaluators operate in democratic societies. In this sense deliberation in evaluation will fit the conception of democracy anticipated, at least roughly.

Or, to turn the notion around, evaluators encourage certain democratic practices by anticipating certain conditions of reception. In other words, some conceptions of evaluation are compatible with particular conceptions of democracy, at least in terms of logical consistency. (We will try to substantiate these claims by considering specific cases in later chapters. Evaluation in nondemocratic societies requires different rationales altogether.)

How might we think about objective value claims in a democracy? The general concept of democracy is that it is a form of government that includes all legitimate interests in reaching governing decisions. Of course, this broad concept of democracy still leaves considerable room for different specific conceptions. Gutmann (1987) identifies a further central requirement of democracy as fostering joint deliberation by citizens on matters of social policy: "conscious social reproduction." Unless every citizen is able to participate meaningfully in this activity, political decision making falls short of the ideal democracy. When only a few decide social policy, an aristocracy, plutocracy, or technocracy exists, depending on whether talent, money, or expertise is the source of authority.

Gutmann's ideal of participatory democracy is a demanding one, and it can never be fully realized in practice. But there are more and less promising ways of approaching it. The conception of democracy that we want to endorse is one in which reflective deliberation takes place that is unbiased and impartial, that leads to unbiased (objective, impartial) conclusions. To arrive at impartial claims the studies must meet certain requirements, in our view: inclusion, dialogue, and deliberation. First, the perceptions and interests of all citizens should be included in decision making about social policy, either directly, through participation, or indirectly, through representation. Second, these perceptions and interests should emerge through dialogical processes in which evaluators pay attention to insider views and interests. And, third, these processes should be deliberative. Perceptions and interests should not be taken at face value but worked back and forth to arrive at the most defensible conclusions.

In our view, it is not enough that participants simply register their opinions and preferences. Their views and preferences should be subject to critique and rational analysis. Nor is it enough that policy makers or researchers decide what the views and preferences of participants are without conducting sufficient dialogue with those participants. Insufficient dialogue can lead to paternalism and getting the views and preferences of participants wrong. This is especially a risk where complex policies and programs are involved and where the powerless and voiceless are stakeholders. Again, a robust democracy requires inclusion, dialogue, and deliberation.

We analyze three other conceptions of democracy in this book that differ from the deliberative democratic conception. These conceptions have tendencies to result in biased findings in different ways. What we call *emotive democracy* draws a sharp line between fact and value claims, then confines rational analysis and objectivity to factual claims only, so construed. In this view, value claims and preferences can receive no cognitive support but are accepted as more or less given. Evaluation may be limited to conditional statements: "If you value X, then do Y."

In this view, deliberation becomes a process in which interest groups win assent to their own policy preferences, with all interests treated as self-regarding "special interests." The strength of this view is that it does resemble the way our political system seems to operate currently—that is, as competition among interest groups. So this view anticipates conditions of receptivity that exist much of the time. The trouble with this conception is that it tends to support the status quo. It inadvertently gives those in power a large advantage because they are in the best position to advance their interests in the competition among interests. Presumably, advocates of this conception would say this is just the way the political world operates, even if it is unfortunate.

Another conception of democracy takes all claims, so-called fact and value claims alike, as being equal. *Hyper-egalitarianism* dismisses authority and expertise altogether, including the expertise of evaluators and social researchers. Participants not only have equal rights to have their claims heard, they have equal rights to have their claims accepted, regardless of what those claims might be. In a sense, all claims are constructed equally, and it doesn't matter whether these are factual or value claims, in this view.

Deliberation in this conception does have the customary aim of reaching agreement on the conclusions to be drawn, but because all claims are equally acceptable, appealing to truth or objectivity to determine the worth of the claims is barred. In fact, in some versions there is no objective truth or external reality to appeal to, only individual constructions.

Hyper-egalitarianism does have the motive of empowering participants on equal terms, an important consideration for full deliberation and dialogue, thus giving the powerless a chance to register their claims. However, the deliberative process in this conception seems to lack rational standards for assessing the content of the claims themselves. Again, inadvertently, powerful stakeholders may dominate because evaluators have no authority to adjudicate participant views. Indeed, they are the same as other participants. Thus, impartial deliberation leading to unbiased conclusions may be thwarted by the interests of the powerful once again.

A third conception of democracy is derived from postmodernism. It promotes diversity of expression as the highest goal—*hyper-pluralism*. Based on the perception that all "regimes of truth" established by authorities privilege some groups and marginalize others, this conception encourages an indefinite proliferation of difference. The emphasis is on encouraging and enabling the expression of different perspectives, with no check on such proliferation. Checking different views to arrive at a "correct" conclusion would inhibit some participants. Standards of truth and objectivity are viewed with suspicion as merely promulgating special interests.

In hyper-pluralism, magnifying differences is seen as disrupting the official and oppressive regimes of truth and thus as liberating. This conception might be considered "postdemocratic," because democracy presumes governance through joint deliberation, constrained by some set of shared procedural rules. Hyper-pluralism has no way of constraining debate and deliberation. Unlimited diversity is the future of postmodern society, postmodernists might reply.

In our view, hyper-pluralism does not seem to lead to governance at all, or to democracy as we understand it. Nor does it provide a very satisfactory basis for evaluation. It is difficult to envision an evaluation practice that serves mainly to disrupt and deconstruct, though some advocates have advanced more constructive roles for postmodern evaluation (e.g., Stronach & MacLure, 1997).

Whichever democratic context is anticipated shapes significantly how studies are conducted and presented. The context of the study restricts the fact-value claims reached by evaluators in different ways and sometimes leads away from unbiased, impartial findings. Inclusion, dialogue, and deliberation are inhibited from arriving at impartial conclusions.

Before examining these ideas in more detail, we turn in the next chapter to an explanation of how evaluators arrive at legitimate evaluative conclusions in general, so that no mystery attaches to how value claims are determined by professionals. The process is a matter of reasoning and empirical evidence sanctioned by the evaluation community.

2

EVALUATIVE REASONING

————•◆•————

ow do evaluators arrive at evaluative conclusions legitimately? Drawing on Scriven's (1980, 1991) formulation, the basic proposition for evaluation is "X is good (bad)," or its derivatives, "X is better (worse) than Y" or "X is worth this much" or "These parts of X are good." Sometimes the evaluative conclusion may not use the word *good* or *bad.* Other words or phrases may do the job in certain specific circumstances. That is, the evaluative conclusion is derived partly from the context in which the statement is made. For example, "This car drives like a dream" is an evaluative statement when it is made in the right context, although the words used are not typical evaluative words.

Again, contingent on the context, in typical usage, "New York is unlivable" is an evaluative statement. "Unlivable" is subject to being defined in concrete terms, such as crowdedness, crime, and expense. The technical philosophical term for the relationship between the evaluative statement and the facts supporting the statement is that the concept of unlivable *subsumes* these other natural, factual conditions. For example, we wouldn't say, "New York is unlivable because it has so many theater performances and art exhibits." That just isn't what we mean by "unlivable." The data and evidence don't fit the concept of "livability."

Now it may be the case that someone says, "New York is unlivable because there are so many art exhibits, I don't know what to do. I wish I lived in Tuscaloosa." Such an idiosyncratic interpretation does not change what we mean by "unlivable" ordinarily. It will also be the case that many people say they would not want to live anywhere else, that New York is not too crowded, or too expensive, or too crime-ridden. Although people may differ on whether they agree with the assessment, that does not make the judgment subjective or incapable of being subjected to evidence.

Rather, it means that the evaluator's task is not an easy one and that many evaluative judgments are contestable by their nature. There will be evidence on both sides. To justify such claims, the evaluator would have to collect data about most people or the representative person or the people who are the recipients of the program under review. The perspective of a billionaire who lives high in a skyscraper protected by security guards would be excluded as the typical perspective from which to make the judgment.

Nor would the evaluator be likely to conclude, "New York is a great city from the criminal's point of view," though that well may be the case. Of course, if the evaluator were hired by the Mafia to provide a rating of cities most suitable to crime, that judgment would be appropriate—or would it? Do evaluators have an obligation only to those who commission the study or pay for it? Or do they have obligations to society as well? After all, the Mafia would pay well, though we might be concerned about their reaction to disappointing evaluation results. The evaluator's social obligation is complex, a point we discuss later.

An evaluative conclusion can be arrived at easily in some cases and only with difficulty in others. In daily life an evaluative statement may express an unsupported opinion without the speaker's presenting evidence. "Good movie. Let's get a drink" requires no evidence, specification, or justification. In professional evaluation, however, the evaluator must present an argument that contains supporting evidence, and this evidence may be weak or strong and may assume a variety of forms. Normally, the argument must be consistent with the definition of evaluation as the determination of the merit, worth, or value of something, specifying the criteria employed in the evaluation and their justification, if need be (Scriven, 1980).

The commonly accepted formulation of the general logic, as delineated by Fournier (1995), drawing on Scriven's work, consists of four idealized steps:

1. Establishing criteria of merit

2. Constructing standards

3. Measuring performance and comparing it to standards

4. Synthesizing and integrating data into judgments of merit

(However, see Stake's holistic counterformulation: "Judgment is the natural avenue to determination of value"; Stake et al., 1997, p. 99.)

Consider evaluation of a product. The criteria for the evaluation must be derived substantially from the nature of the product itself and from the function the product is designed to serve. There are certain characteristics of the product that exist objectively, for example, a car's drivability, safety, and cost. Of course, these criteria depend on human use of some kind, so they are relative to that, but they are objective in the sense that they can be determined by consideration of evidence. In product evaluation, evaluators posit a typical user, sometimes implicitly, without trying to determine the full range of uses to which the product might be put. Rather, criteria are established with reference to the typical consumer of the product. So the safety of a car is determined under "normal use" conditions. In a sense much of the context is determined.

Now, a skeptic might say, "I want my car to pull my boat, which happens to be a J-class racing vessel. None of these cars will do the job." Fair enough. Such people have special uses in mind, but such special uses are not how cars are normally used, and we would not say that cars are no good because they don't fulfill these special functions. Nor would we say the evaluation was not objective because it did not consider these criteria. The criteria are objective in the sense that they are based on the needs of the typical consumer, not that they meet every conceivable need of any potential consumer.

This is a major theme. Just because we can conceive, imagine, or fantasize special conditions or purposes to which a product or program can be put, that does not mean the evaluation must take into account any and all such conditions. The product does not have to satisfy every conceivable need in order for the evaluation to be objective. Rather, it is the typical use and user that count in most cases. Philosophers have a habit of trying to universalize everything. In the world of the practical, where evaluators live, it is neither necessary nor desirable to accommodate all possibilities, as the imaginary world of logical possibility would demand.

It is a matter of fact about the object under investigation whether it possesses certain properties and ministers to certain needs, wants, desires, and aims. And this determination depends on whether the criteria selected are the right criteria for the evaluation. Plugged in someplace is the idea that the product or whatever satisfies some human need or concern. It is an objective fact whether the object does so or not.

However, knowing the purpose of a car, for instance, is not enough from which to derive criteria such as safety, comfort, and reliability. To derive these, one must consider other human aims, such as the urge to live without injury. And there is nothing subjective or arbitrary about such criteria, except in the sense that they attend to human needs or wants. It is an objective fact that certain cars are safer than others, given human characteristics and evidence in the form of safety statistics perhaps.

Of course, sometimes the criteria may conflict with each other, so that we must arrive at judgments after reflection. Safer cars may be heavier and more damaging to the environment. Conclusions cannot be read off automatically, as one would read a thermometer. Often, we must distinguish between criteria that are important and those less so, even if all are appropriate. In automobile evaluations this winnowing is done through a narrowing of the field of comparison to cars of a certain kind or cost (domain restriction) or through ratings of the cars on all relevant criteria so that consumers can make their own judgments about which criteria are most important.

EVALUATION AUDIENCES AND STAKEHOLDERS

There is a serious complication to the logic of evaluation. Suppose that we are evaluating a science education program supported by the National Science Foundation. It is not only the nature of the program we need consider when arriving at the appropriate criteria. We might want to justify the program to Congress, the source of funding. We might want to tell program participants themselves what is going on. Or we might want to tell managers at NSF which of their programs are working.

Each of these audiences requires different information. Although some information may be useful for all, Congress wants to know about the "impacts" of the program—the number of teachers involved, number of students affected, the amount test scores were raised. Program managers would like to know which parts of their programs are working and which are not, so they can change things. NSF officials want to know how they can shift funds into more successful programs. Now, we might imagine all potential audiences and construct an evaluation for each, but again this is the real world, and who has the resources to conduct such evaluations? Also, it would be wasteful to do so, even if we had the resources. Why collect data for imaginary audiences?

We can also distinguish between audiences and stakeholders. Audiences are those who read the evaluation report and may use the findings somehow, whereas stakeholders are those whose interests are at stake in the product, program, or policy. Often, audiences are stakeholders. But some stakeholders may never read the report, even though their interests may be vitally at stake, such as children in educational programs or patients in medical programs. Yet probably their interests should be paramount. Every group whose interests are vitally concerned in some way should be a consideration for the evaluation.

We might think of the evaluator as building arguments for different audiences to show whether the program is successful, arguments in which relevant stakeholder interests are included (House, 1980). Leaving out important stakeholder interests results in an improper evaluation (a biased one). Of course, one strategy might be to collect data that would satisfy all criteria for all audiences. But the resources for any evaluation fall far short of evidence for all possible audiences. So a critical question is, Who are the major audiences and stakeholders for this evaluation? Specifying these goes a long way toward deciding which criteria to employ.

For example, in a case discussed later in detail, Karlsson (1998) conducted an evaluation of social care services in Sweden in which the stakeholders included politicians concerned with economic efficacy, program managers concerned with program control, social service professionals concerned about the guiding principles of care, parents concerned that the professionals were interested in their particular children, and the children themselves concerned about contact with their schoolmates. It would seem that information should be collected about each major group's concern.

Doesn't this make the criteria and evaluation *relative* to the values and preferences of the audiences and stakeholders? To some extent, that is true in the sense that the evaluation is particular and incomplete, not general. It does not include all conceivable criteria, audiences, or stakeholders. Yet the selected audiences and stakeholders are not arbitrary. Not just any audience or stakeholder concern will do. Not just any criterion an audience wants should be included in the evaluation. The nature of the program itself, its function, what it is doing—these are decisive considerations.

Specifying audiences and stakeholders fills in the context of the evaluation, and understanding the context is critical, including the purpose of the evaluation and how the results are likely to be used. Professional evaluation does not occur in a vacuum. It is not evaluation for oneself. Rather, it is a social as well as cognitive process. It entails deriving criteria; collecting, analyzing, and interpreting data; *and* communicating the results to other people. When we construct arguments about whether a program or policy is any good, we are well on the way to designing the evaluation. Where are the loopholes in the argument? What needs to be strengthened to make the argument? What will the main audiences accept as credible evidence? Are the interests of various stakeholder groups considered? Ultimately, the evaluator must put all these considerations together.

Making arguments that others find persuasive doesn't mean that the exercise is merely rhetorical. Presumably, the argument reflects the reality of the situation, even though audiences may differ among themselves on what facts and arguments they find most persuasive. For example, program participants may well find intensive interviews with a few students persuasive evidence of the critical thinking in mathematics they are seeking, whereas Congress is unlikely to find a few informal interviews convincing. But both the informal interviews and more formal indicators reflect the reality of program achievement, just different aspects of it.

POINTS OF VIEW

Let's put the matter (perhaps too) philosophically. There is a difference between "good of a kind X," which means the thing fulfills a role, and "good from a Y point of view," which means it affects the interests of Y (Urmson, 1968). We might say, "This is a good road," which means it has the characteristics that good roads should have.

The road is straight and smooth. This is an evaluation of "good of a kind," most often seen in product evaluations.

However, consider "This road is a good thing from the farmer's point of view." Having the road means that the farmers can get their produce to market easily, but this says little about the quality or characteristics of the road as a road, a thing of its kind. Rather, the existence of the road is good from the farmers' perspective (it suits their particular interests). When we have products, programs, or policies that serve interests differentially, the evaluation is "good from a perspective"—a stakeholder's perspective.

Both points of view are common in professional evaluation, but there are confusions between them sometimes. Often we hear evaluators arguing that the object under review has certain characteristics or functions (a medical program is supposed to cure patients) and others arguing that criteria must come from the perspectives of stakeholder groups (serve their interests). In fact, we can do both in an evaluation and both in a single evaluation through employment of multiple criteria. The evaluation becomes a blending of the characteristics of the entity and the interests of stakeholders.

Of course, there is a sense in which these come together. The characteristics of a good road are those that the typical driver would want in a road. Things of a kind serve a typical or implicit user. Good from a perspective also serves interests, but those that are more special and particular. The "point of view" becomes especially important in complex entities that have differential effects on different groups.

To complicate matters further, there can be very abstract points of view—agricultural, economic, political, aesthetic (Taylor, 1961), and so on; for example, "This is not a good policy from an agricultural point of view." Somehow a point of view has been developed around an institution. We can derive criteria based on what's good from an agricultural point of view, which is more abstract than the point of view of farmers. "The New Zealand export policy is good from an agricultural point of view"—that is, the view that promotes the interests of agriculture.

Although this may look tangential for evaluation, it is not. Many programs and policies are judged from an economic point of view, without regard to the interests of more specific groups. Furthermore, economic criteria are regularly employed in evaluation without explicit justification. It is assumed that economic considerations should be important. We might speculate that this reflects the pervasive influence of economic institutions in society as a whole, just as we might speculate that religious points of view will not be applied in contemporary professional evaluation.

The general point of view taken may obscure the interests of the groups that benefit. "Good from an agricultural point of view" may mean that large farmers benefit but not small ones. There can be conflicting interests among stakeholder groups. We avoid this problem in product evaluation by taking the typical consumer's interest as paramount, making the choice between the consumer's and the producer's interests clear. There is a big difference between a good car from the consumer's point of view and a good car from the viewpoint of General Motors.

In program and policy evaluation the notion of conflicting interests is even more pressing: Different programs and policies can have differential benefits for different groups, a major reason the evaluation community has developed the concept of stakeholder evaluation (Bryk, 1983; Weiss, 1983). Defining the appropriate criteria becomes an evolving part of the evaluation.

In summary, there are at least these possibilities for deriving criteria:

❐ Inspect the product, program, or policy.

❐ Consult accepted evaluation models.

❐ Ask potential audiences, including clients.

❐ Ask stakeholders.

❐ Consider institutional points of view.

❏ Determine needs of recipients.

❏ Consider the context of the program and evaluation.

❏ Consult the research literature on the subject.

❏ Consider social theories, such as those of justice and gender.

In fact, Rogers and Owen (1995) have identified numerous potential sources of evaluative criteria, and it is difficult to dismiss any of them.

How can we manage all these? How can we possibly put all these considerations together? There are formal and informal ways of doing so. The formal ways take the form of the rules and procedures that the evaluation community has adopted as guidelines—guidelines that have been debated within the community over time. These include the evaluation models and methods of data collection and analysis. This formal knowledge is the basis for evaluator training. Newer guidelines include ethical standards. There is less agreement on deriving criteria or combining results. These procedures have not undergone formalization or rigorous scrutiny. In these cases, we resort mostly to informal reasoning.

AN EXAMPLE

Imagine an evaluation of an educational program, a third-grade literacy program based on holistic instruction. On the one hand, the evaluator must be concerned about short-term versus long-term results. The program might produce enjoyment of learning and better language skills, but not result in gains on standardized reading tests compared with more structured programs, especially those keyed to the content and procedures of the tests. The evaluator knows from visiting the site that the continuation of the program depends on the evaluation's assuring the governing board that the program is working. Board members want results, and perhaps the state tests will show their schools are not performing as well as those in nearby school districts. The parents are anxious about their children learning to read quickly.

The evaluator must discover and keep these things in mind. She might reason that it would be wise to use different measures of success, some attuned to long-term and some to short-term learning. The statewide test is mandated, so there is one likely measure. The evaluator might inspect the test to see what kinds of items are used and how these reflect the reading program. To balance this measure with others, samples of student work, graded by a panel of teachers, might provide an indication of more holistic learning outcomes. Interviews with parents, students, and teachers might provide an idea of how enthusiastic the children are about the program. How much do they read at home? How much do parents help? To what extent are their actions compatible with holistic learning?

When results from these data collection procedures are combined, they may well contain conflicting information. Perhaps the test scores of the students are slightly worse than those from the rest of the district. Can this be explained by past performance or factors such as social class? Can it be explained by the content of the test as it relates to program content? On the other hand, perhaps the student work is judged superior in performance compared with the work of other students, and parents report that their children are enthusiastic about the class and that they help their children more at home with reading tasks. As the evaluator analyzes such information, she must develop ideas about how these things fit together. Many considerations involve particular facts and criteria. Just how good is the student work? Just how enthusiastic are the parents? Just how bad are the test scores? How good are the tests themselves? How important overall is long-term versus short-term performance in this case?

Because these factors are largely locally determined and interact strongly with other local factors, the determination of the worth of the program depends heavily on the context. In fact, it is much easier to make judgments in context, when we have specific, concrete information. In the concrete situation, we can make a reasonable judgment about how these various factors work together to produce the results that they do. In another situation these factors might interact in different ways. Perhaps other teachers would not be so involved, or perhaps the test content would be different, or perhaps the aspirations of the parents would differ.

In tying these things together, the evaluator constructs an account of the specific situation, which involves weighting criteria, facts, and interests, even when these things conflict with one another. In other words, the evaluator works to produce a coherent account of the situation in evaluative terms. Such an account is not a general statement about the worth of holistic reading instruction everywhere; rather, it is a statement about the worth of this program at this time and place, in these circumstances.

Hence, the evaluation produced is particular. Its generalizability to other contexts is contingent on factors in other settings and problematic because of the difficulty of identifying and accounting for interacting factors. Generalizability is more than a sampling problem; it is a substantive problem as well. Not only are different factors relevant in different contexts, but the weights assigned to different factors may change with each context to some degree. The evaluation can be disputed if it can be shown that the evaluator did not take some important fact or criterion into consideration, so that the account is spuriously coherent, or that the evaluator weighted factors improperly, so that another account is more coherent. Evaluations cannot eliminate conflicts. Rather, evaluations produce the best judgments we can arrive at in the situation, given the conflicts.

Consider another example. Which is better, short-term or long-term training? In this form, this evaluation question is hardly answerable. What kind of training, for whom, for what purpose, toward what ends, at what expense? The context is lacking, and without a context, the issue is too open to evaluate. Somehow a context must be defined; for example, "The National Science Foundation is thinking about funding summer training institutes for teachers in math and science, and the issue is whether 2-week or 8-week workshops would be best." Specifications and limitations provided by the context make an evaluation possible. Otherwise, the problem is so open-ended and concerned with so many possibilities that it is indeterminate.

DELIBERATION IN CONTEXT

The general notion is that evaluators work within context to produce an overall evaluation that provides coherence from the information available from various sources. Through substantive deliberation, a process of dealing with particular facts, criteria, and interests in context, evaluators can produce a determination of the merit or worth of programs, policies, and personnel (Hurley, 1989).

Two key ideas involve producing the evaluation in a given context and producing an evaluation that is coherent. In general, the best evaluation is one that brings everything together most coherently. However, if the evaluator has achieved coherence by omitting important relevant criteria or facts, then the evaluation can be disputed. Of course, no account can ever be perfectly coherent, because the evaluator must deal with conflicting criteria and interests.

There is not necessarily one dominant criterion that the evaluator can appeal to, though one may arise in the course of the study. Rather, the evaluator must make do with the specific criteria and facts within the concrete situation. Indeed, it is the limitation of the context that enables the evaluator to make such judgments successfully. Consideration of particular facts and criteria facilitates sound judgment because it limits possibilities that might make a determination of worth impossibly complex.

The deliberative process has several stages (Hurley, 1989). First, we bring basic concepts to bear. For the evaluator this means discovering which criteria apply—not always easy. The evaluator examines the situation to achieve a grasp of the issues, including which are relevant. Guidelines suggest what criteria must be considered. For example, one might be "Consider the views of the major stakeholders in the evaluation"; another, "Relate criteria to the goals of the program"; and another, "Analyze the program goals."

Such considerations are general ones derived from the evaluation community. Professional evaluators share concepts and practices, including established evaluation models and data collection procedures, that they have learned through education, experience, and professional affiliation. Based on such knowledge, they look to see which concepts and practices apply. Alternatives and comparisons depend on the discovery and illumination of different aspects of the evaluation. Testing and student performance, long-term and short-term payoffs, school boards and parents are all familiar concepts to educational evaluators.

Another phase of deliberation involves specifying the content of these general considerations. Exactly who are the major stakeholders in this case? What are the goals of the program? What outcomes can be expected? These considerations involve particular facts in particular contexts for particular people. So the evaluator derives a design by surveying facts to see which deserve consideration and determining the relative weight of these considerations.

If the elements fit together, there may be no need to go further, but often there are conflicts. The parents and the school board may want different things. Parents may want their children to write well, but the school board may want higher test scores. In conflict situations, it may be useful for evaluators to articulate the criteria, principles, and purposes that inform practices. Part of the weighing and balancing may involve thinking about examples from other cases. How have long-term and short-term results been balanced in other studies? How has the field handled similar cases? How have such evaluations been criticized in the past? Knowledge of studies of similar programs can be helpful.

We develop the concepts for criteria by defining performance in detail. How is performance to be judged and measured? The evaluator examines relationships among criteria and data, perhaps subordinating some to others, perhaps referring to previous studies or analogies with other situations in order to determine relationships among criteria. Eventually, the evaluator forms ideas about the relationships among the various elements. If the test scores are somewhat lower than those of a comparison group but the holistic scoring indicates that the students' writing products are better, does she say that the program is successful? The evaluator must balance short-term results with long-term results and differently measured results with each other. How will each be weighted?

On the other hand, specific information provides constraints. How good are these particular teachers in implementing this program? How much commitment is there? The evaluator gathers data, generates ideas about relationships among criteria and works out the best possible combination. Finally, she arrives at an overall synthesis judgment, highly qualified in most cases. (And, of course, the process is messier than this idealized reasoning process would suggest.)

For the most part, these considerations are based on substantive concerns, on matters of specific content rather than formal procedures. On the one hand, there are practices the evaluator has inherited. These apply in most situations, and they provide the evaluator with starting points in terms of what determinations are legitimate. On the other hand, the evaluator must know details about the setting and the program in operation in order to make informed judgments. Once she knows these details, she can see more clearly which of the possible designs, measures, and data collection procedures make sense.

The evaluator is able to take relevant multiple criteria and interests and combine them into all-things-considered judgments in which everything is consolidated and related. She combines test scores with interview data, short-term with long-term learning, the interests of parents with those of the school board with those of the children.

To accomplish this, the evaluator must make judgments. Like a referee in a ball game, the evaluator must follow certain sets of rules, procedures, and considerations—not just anything goes. Although judgment is involved, it is judgment exercised within the constraints of the setting and accepted practices. Two different evaluators might make different determinations, as might two referees, but acceptable interpretations are limited. In the sense that there is room for the evaluator to employ judgment, the deliberative process is individual. In the sense that the situation is constrained, the judgment is professional—which is not to deny that some evaluators may be better at it than others.

There is disagreement among evaluators about how systematic the final synthesis of an evaluation can be. For example, Scriven (1994) asserts that evaluative reasoning can be reduced to three steps—testing, validation, and synthesis—with standard procedures for arriving at "probative inferences" (conclusions that are plausible, given no strong countervailing evidence). On the other hand, Stake et al. (1997) find such claims too rule governed. They see "perceptual judgment" as being a critical part of evaluation. The evaluator experiences the quality of something and works to explicate, elaborate, and represent this quality in the report. But conclusions are not rendered by standardized procedures. Judgment comes first, standards later.

In either case, evaluators must make many judgments about what to do for which there are no clear professional rules. It is difficult to see how this could be otherwise, regardless of which approach to evaluation is employed. For evaluators, personal responsibility is a cost of doing business, just as it is for physicians, who must make dozens of clinical judgments each day and hope for the best. The rules and procedures of no profession are explicit enough to prevent this. The elimination of bias is done by external review.

So this is our first approximation of how legitimate professional value claims are produced. We expand on this later, in Part III. Before that, in Part II we critique how other evaluation theorists differ on how they conceive the fact-value distinction, how they handle the connection between evaluation and democracy, and how they treat the role of the evaluator.

PART II

Critiques of Other Views

THE RECEIVED VIEW

———•◆•———

he "received view" has been the dominant view of the role of values in evaluation since it emerged as a distinct field in the 1960s. The received view endorses a version of the fact-value dichotomy, although we hasten to add that this does not imply that its proponents are positivists. Indeed, some are staunchly opposed to the positivist conception of knowledge. Still, embracing the fact-value dichotomy even in attenuated form misconstrues the role of values in evaluation and may lead to less-than-ideal practices.

We focus our analysis on Campbell (1974, 1982) and Shadish, Cook, and Leviton (1995) as our primary exemplars of the received view, though other evaluation theorists also qualify as adherents of that view. Let us say at the beginning that these theorists have produced some of the finest work in evaluation. In critiquing their stands on values, we have chosen the best scholars as exemplars and do not mean to question their overall contributions to the field. Rather, we want to question only one aspect of their work, their perspective on values.

Here is a sketch of the argument of this chapter. Campbell rejected the tenets of positivism by insisting there is no foundational structure to knowledge, no pure observation that might substantiate or refute knowledge claims. Rather, knowledge claims had to be tested against the general body of other knowledge propositions to see if they were consistent.

However, Campbell (1974, 1982) saw values as quite different. He explicitly adhered to the fact-value dichotomy, claiming we cannot argue rationally about values but rather must either accept or reject them on some undetermined grounds. Hence, when it comes to evaluating programs, evaluators can determine only whether the program worked or worked better than others relative to some goal (value); there is no way for evaluators to examine the underlying values rationally. In this sense, value claims are epistemologically different from knowledge claims.

Clearly, this position limits the acceptable scope of evaluation. Not being able to criticize goals or underlying premises places severe constraints on evaluators. The most important aspects of programs and policies might go unexamined. In our view of facts and values, evaluators can examine the goals and values of the program or policies they evaluate—and in practice they often do so.

There is also a newer version of the received view. Shadish et al. (1995) argue more from practical (rather than epistemological) grounds. They contend that as a practical matter there is too much disagreement about values for evaluators to be able to arrive at accepted value conclusions. Furthermore, if evaluators did arrive at substantive value conclusions, policy makers and others would not accept these claims as legitimate. They would think evaluators were imposing their personal views rather than acting as professionals.

Hence, evaluators should divide value statements into *descriptive valuing* and *prescriptive valuing*. With descriptive valuing, evaluators mostly report the values of others about the programs and policies under review. Prescriptive valuing, arriving at explicit value conclusions based on substantive values, should be used sparingly, only where significant value agreement exists. In practice, the best that evaluators can hope to do in most cases is to arrive at conclusions such as "If you value Y, then X is the case." Evaluators provide each major stakeholder group with information about the programs and policies that promote the values to which the group subscribes without the evaluators' "prescribing" those values.

We call this second version of the received view *value minimalism*. Value minimalism stops short of the extreme view historically associated with positivism, *value freedom*, which is based on the strict fact-value dichotomy. Adherents of value minimalism admit that *some* values are essential in evaluation. For example, they accept the idea that professions such as evaluation must have ethical standards. In fact, Shadish has been instrumental in developing such standards for the American Evaluation Association. Nonetheless, such valuing should be held to a minimum, in his view.

We believe that value minimalism is rooted in two underlying theses: (a) the radical undecidability of values and (b) the emotive (or preferential) conception of democracy. The first thesis is that there is simply too much disagreement about societal values for them to serve as a basis for evaluation. The second thesis concerns the type of democracy that evaluation serves, a particular view of how stakeholder interests should be registered and handled.

By contrast, we argue against the thesis that values are undecidable by claiming that many evaluative statements are blends of facts and values that are often impossible to untangle and that it is not easy to separate descriptive from prescriptive valuing. These also blend together. Rather, evaluators can arrive at evaluative conclusions by attending to the procedures of professional evaluation. However, these procedures should include a specific value framework from which to operate, one that must be justified.

First, we challenge the view that facts and value statements can be separated from one another very precisely or that descriptions only describe. In certain contexts, such as evaluation reports, descriptions of settings, programs, and policies are neither value-neutral nor purely descriptive; rather, they are often actually evaluative within the context of the report. Indeed, evaluators play upon their abilities to use descriptions to fortify evaluative conclusions. And, conversely, evaluative statements often are descriptive ones as well.

Second, we challenge the argument that because there is so much disagreement on values, the practical solution is to present conditional value summaries ("X is good if you value Y"). Shadish et al. contend that it is not practical for evaluators to present more conclusive value claims because policy makers know there is endemic value disagreement. Otherwise, evaluators would not be listened to.

Our counterargument is that practicality by itself is not a sufficient justification for evaluation. We must ask, Practical for what? Something could be practical for bad ends. Using practicality as the primary criterion for evaluation means evaluators may serve whatever ends clients or policy makers endorse. Evaluation should be premised on higher social goals than being useful to those in power. (Of course, it is not enough to criticize practicality as an end; we must say what we think those social ends are.) We turn now to the detailed arguments that characterize the received view of values, arguments worth very serious consideration.

THE RADICAL UNDECIDABILITY THESIS

The radical undecidability thesis holds that pervasive disagreement is endemic to values and cannot be eliminated. Associated with this thesis are ways both to account for the disagreement and to deal with it. Although distinguishable, these two aspects are not easy to disentangle. First we deal with accounting for disagreement.

Accounting for the Undecidability of Values

One of the clearest and most concise accounts of undecidability in values is provided by the great pioneering evaluation theorist Donald Campbell (1982):

The tools of descriptive science and formal logic can help us implement values which we already accept or have chosen, but they are not constitutive of those values. Ultimate values are accepted but not justified. (p. 123)

Campbell explicitly embraces the fact-value distinction of "the logical positivists and their predecessors" (p. 123). Like the positivists, he perceives a sizable epistemological gap between descriptive science on the one hand and values on the other. Values are undecidable because they have no cognitive basis; they must be "chosen" and "accepted" and cannot be "justified." They cannot be treated rationally, studied, discussed, and determined.

What is the basis for the epistemological difference between facts and values according to positivism? We provide a fuller characterization of positivism's conception of values in the next chapter. It is sufficient for our purposes here to note that the conception of values is derived from positivism's central tenet of *verifiability*: In order for a claim to qualify as legitimate knowledge, in order for it to be "cognitively significant," the claim has to be testable either in terms of direct observation or in terms of formal logic. (Note the parallel to Campbell's "tools of descriptive science and formal logic.")

Because value claims cannot be verified (or falsified) in either of these ways, they were deemed by positivists to be lacking in cognitive content—not knowledge claims at all, but rather disguised expressions of emotions. Thus, the gap between facts and values characteristic of positivism is a corollary of its general epistemology, not an independent thesis in its own right. That the positivist fact-value distinction is a corollary of positivism's epistemology creates an inconsistency in Campbell's overall view.

Campbell was an early and effective critic of positivism in social research. He endorsed the view, generally shared since Kuhn's *Structure of Scientific Revolutions* (1962), that positivism's verifiability criterion is untenable. There is no way to isolate empirical data totally from theoretical concepts and frameworks. Instead, data and concepts are always intermingled such that scientific knowledge is always "theory-laden" or, as Campbell (1974) puts it, "presumptive."

Verification and falsification are holistic on this view: Claims are tested against one another for coherence and consistency, and some of them are (unavoidably) presumed. Factual claims are tested against the larger body of facts. Viewed another way, there are always claims, including factual claims, that must be "accepted but not justified" in scientific research. So Campbell's notion that values must be "accepted but not justified" does not distinguish values from knowledge claims in general. Some facts must also be accepted in this postpositivist view.

Campbell seems not to have recognized the tight connection between positivism's epistemological stance and its stance on values, not to have recognized that to abandon the epistemology is to abandon the corollary fact-value distinction, in order to be consistent. Without the verifiability criterion to judge things by, just as facts cannot be isolated from theory, facts cannot be isolated from values, either. Thus, just as facts are theory-laden, they are value-laden as well (at least in social research).

In light of these connections, if a rigid fact-value distinction is to be preserved, some independent, nonpositivist analysis or justification is required. Campbell does not provide one, to our knowledge. On the contrary, he explicitly aligns himself with the positivist analysis and the rigid fact-value distinction. Actually, we doubt that an independent defense of the fact-value distinction is tenable.

But rather than canvass and critique all possibilities, we provide an alternative account of values, one fully consistent with postpositivist epistemology. Our own account emerges throughout this book. Our general conception is that evaluators not only are able to document the goals and values of programs and policies, but can and should critically examine goals and values as part of evaluations. Fact and value claims can be tested against the larger holistic body of fact-value claims. Such a view leads to somewhat different practices and roles for evaluators than those advocated by Campbell.

A more recent version of the received view is to be found in the influential book *Foundations of Program Evaluation*, by Shadish et al. (1995). Paralleling Campbell's descriptive science/values distinction, Shadish et al. distinguish "descriptive valuing" from "prescriptive valuing." In descriptive valuing, evaluators confine themselves to describing the values held by different stakeholders; in prescriptive valuing, evaluators incorporate and advance their own substantive value positions—for example, a particular conception of justice (e.g., House, 1980).

Shadish et al. contend that evaluators should confine themselves to description primarily, but rather than give an account along *epistemological lines* à la Campbell (that because values cannot be justified, evaluators cannot legitimately advance value judgments), they give an account more or less along *practical lines* (that because value disagreement is rife in society, it is not practical for evaluators to advance value judgments). We turn to practicality in the next section, but first we pursue the question of whether Shadish et al. can avoid being committed to the epistemological gulf between science (descriptive valuing) and values (prescriptive valuing) that characterizes Campbell's view, given other features of their position.

Shadish et al. include separate sections in their seminal book on the "knowledge" versus the "value" "components of evaluation theory," indirect evidence that they embrace an epistemological gap between facts and values. The implication is that knowledge and values are different kinds of things. Further evidence is the descriptive/prescriptive distinction. They give repeated warnings about the inadvisability of prescriptive valuing on the grounds that it is plagued with disagreement, unlike descriptive valuing.

Such a stance does not *necessarily* entail an epistemological gulf between description and prescription. It might merely be a fact about prescriptive valuing to be dealt with practically. But because Shadish et al. are committed to the view that it is possible to describe things without also prescribing them, they also seem to be committed to a version of the fact-value dichotomy at some implicit level. Otherwise, the distinction between descriptive and prescriptive valuing could not serve its function of allowing (requiring) evaluators to identify and remove their own substantive value commitments, leaving only the descriptive components. In other words, an epistemological gap seems to exist between description and valuing in their view.

This is a shaky foundation on which to erect a theory of evaluation. The idea that description (descriptive valuing) and evaluation (prescriptive valuing) can be successfully separated has been convincingly undermined by philosophers over the past decades. To make this point another way, just as description is theory-laden, it is also value-laden. To be sure, many isolated claims can be virtually value-free—for example, "2 + 2 = 4"; "The cat is on the mat"; "George Washington was the first president of the United States." But it is mistaken to conclude from these examples that a sharp epistemological dividing line exists between description and evaluation. Where knowledge is squared with the contemporary, holistic epistemology associated with notions such as "paradigms" and "conceptual schemes," context and background knowledge become all-important in the interpretation of the meanings of statements.

Thus, we can imagine the sentence "George Washington was the first president of the United States," uttered in a certain place at a certain time, against a certain background, as being highly evaluative. For instance, suppose in the flow of a conversation it becomes known that George Washington was a white male and a slave owner. "George Washington was the first president of the United States" can then be used to evaluate the country's beginnings negatively—for example, as patriarchal and racist. The general point, as Scriven (1969) observes, is that

> there is no ultimate factual language. And the more interesting side of the coin is that many statements which in one context would clearly be evaluational are, in another, clearly factual. Obvious examples include judgments of intelligence

and the merit of performances such as those of runners in the Olympic Games. (p. 199)

Similarly, in an evaluation we may start off with what seem to be simple facts and descriptions, but these descriptions often serve the evaluative conclusions that are to follow in the report. The evaluator has selected the description to bolster the evaluative conclusions to come later. For example, recall how Stake's (1995) description of an elementary school in Chicago fits coherently with his evaluative conclusions. In this context the description of the school has evaluative implications that are deliberately honed, even if the text is simultaneously descriptive as well. The descriptive-evaluative passages are key parts of the report, even if readers only later grasp the full implications of Stake's message. Indeed, all skilled qualitative investigators work this way. Their studies would not be coherent and effective if they did not.

The key here is how the context determines the evaluative message of the text. What seems descriptive in one context becomes not only descriptive but evaluative in another, as with the George Washington example. Furthermore, evaluative content is often an indispensable part of precise description. Compare the following statements:

- ❏ "Jones killed Smith with malice" and "Jones's actions led to Smith's death."

- ❏ "Latino parents are passive in their dealings with school officials" and "Latino parents are unaggressive in their dealings with school officials."

- ❏ "The project director stole $50,000 in project funds" and "The project director deposited $50,000 in project funds into his personal account."

❑ "Gay and lesbian youth are oppressed in public schools" and "Gay and lesbian youth experience disproportionate difficulties in public schools."

In each of these pairs, the first description is more evaluatively laden than the second. But these descriptions are not biased or inaccurate for that reason. Instead, they *describe* different states of affairs and, accordingly, have different truth conditions to satisfy. Changing their evaluative content changes what is being described. What is more, changing their evaluative content expressly to render them more evaluatively neutral can compromise their ability to guide practice (Rorty, 1982). In each of the above pairs, the first description better targets problems and remedies than does the second.

So, again, we believe these statements contain blends of facts and values and are not purely one or the other, or to put it another way, the statements are both descriptive and evaluative at the same time. And many evaluation reports are so structured that even apparent descriptions or apparent evaluative claims contain strong elements of both facts and values, given the context of their use. Our conclusion is that evaluators should acknowledge this intertwining of facts and values.

Dealing With Undecidability

The arguments in the preceding section challenge the epistemological foundation of the fact-value dichotomy. But "de facto" undecidability in the domain of values remains an important issue. That different sets of values are endorsed and advanced (and that we are often unable to resolve disputes about them) leads some proponents of the received view to argue that values should be rooted out, separated from facts, and set to one side as a *practical* matter. Once again, the work of Donald Campbell (1982) is a good place to start in explicating the received view:

An established power structure with the ability to employ applied social scientists, the machinery of social science, and control over the means of dissemination produces an unfair status quo bias in the mass production of belief assertions from the applied social sciences. . . . This state of affairs is one which . . . I deplore, but I find myself best able to express my disapproval through retaining the old-fashioned construct of truth, warnings against clique selfish distortions, and a vigorously exhorted fact-value distinction. (p. 125)

Now, we agree that Campbell identifies a serious problem for social research (as he often does): Imbalances in power can bias social research findings so as to favor certain interests. However, we doubt that facts and values can be wholly disentangled. Thus, there are no value-neutral descriptions of the kind Campbell endorses with his "vigorously exhorted fact-value distinction." Far from eliminating biases, operating with the premise that there can be value-neutral descriptions may introduce disguised forms of bias.

For example, consider the concept of "intelligence" and whether it can be rendered value-neutral. It is hard to imagine intelligence retaining its current interest if it were not identified with something good. As such, its evaluative content accompanies it in the constellation of beliefs, policies, and practices in which it is embedded. The belief that its evaluative content can be eliminated from "descriptive science" only results in the smuggling of values into policy surreptitiously. The alternative is to investigate, evaluate, and debate the consequences of using the concept of intelligence in formulating policy.

For their part, Shadish et al. approach the problem of what to do about de facto undecidability about values largely in terms of practicality. They criticize as impractical those evaluation theorists (especially House and Scriven) who advocate substantive value commitments (prescriptive valuing) on the part of evaluators. The basic contours of Shadish et al.'s argument (reconstructed to explicate premises) are as follows: (a) Undecidability in the value domain is a fact; (b) everyone knows this, including policy makers and stakeholders; (c) incorporating and advancing substantive values in the conduct, findings, and recommendations of an evaluation is prescriptive valuing; (d) given a and b, policy makers and stakeholders will reject evaluations that involve prescriptive valuing on the part of evaluators; (e) therefore, evaluations that incorporate substantive values are impractical.

But what does it mean to say something is impractical? Being practical is not a categorical good—that is, a good in itself. The claim "X is practical (impractical)" is elliptical for "X is practical (impractical) as a means to Y." The "Y" that Shadish et al. seem to have in mind is "having access, being listened to, being taken seriously, and having an influence on policy making." It is understandable that Scriven (1986) rejects such a position as too compromised. It requires evaluators to accept the values and goals of clients and policy makers, whatever they might be. Surely the evaluator would want to be practical only toward some good end, not toward a bad one.

For example, evaluators who evaluate the effects of tobacco are not poor practitioners of their craft, even if the results are ignored because the researchers are accused of bias by the tobacco lobby for doing "prescriptive valuing" based on the adverse health effects of smoking. If "having access, being listened to, being taken seriously, and having an influence on policy making" are the only goals of evaluation, then evaluators may simply serve those who hold the reigns of power, providing support for the status quo that Campbell would oppose.

Shadish et al. qualify their position by saying that *some* prescriptive valuing is sometimes appropriate, and perhaps they would say that the tobacco example is one of those cases. We can think of other endeavors where they might think prescriptive valuing would be justified—those involving health, crime, racism, sexism. They also would include ethical codes of professional conduct among the legitimate varieties of prescriptive valuing. Thus, because Shadish et al.

endorse some prescriptive valuing, we associate their view with value minimalism rather than value freedom. They see some prescriptive valuing as necessary.

But here is the problem: *Once prescriptive valuing is acknowledged as legitimate, some argument is required to show why it should be kept to a minimum or to indicate just how far it should go.* The argument from practicality is not up to the task of justifying such a position, because some further criteria—beyond evaluator influence—are required to interpret Y in the formula "practical as a means to Y." Shadish et al. may be able to produce such an argument, but one is not clear in their book.

Persistence of the Undecidability of Values Thesis

Why does the undecidability of values thesis retain widespread acceptance despite the nearly unanimous repudiation of positivism and value-free social science? Three factors seem to contribute. First, the examples used to support the fact-value dichotomy are unbalanced. Typical examples emphasize value disagreements and ignore value agreements. Second, it is not fully recognized that the sciences themselves have regulative values, such as honesty, without which they could not function. Third, the deep-seated ocular metaphor of knowledge is pervasive.

The putative epistemological gulf between facts and values is often illustrated through the juxtaposition of claims such as "Grass is green" and "Abortion is morally wrong." Wittgenstein (1960) says that we are often led astray by an unbalanced diet of examples. This may be one of those cases. The examples used are insufficiently general. Such examples pick out uncontroversial factual claims and compare them with controversial value claims. To turn it around, compare "Light is composed of waves" and "Torturing children for fun is good." Here is a comparison in which the so-called factual claim is more controversial than the so-called value claim. Choosing

"Abortion is wrong" to establish the undecidability thesis masks the widespread agreement on values that characterizes social life and, indeed, makes social life possible.

In addition to "Don't torture children for fun," consider "Don't gratuitously spit on, punch, or kick a passerby in the shins"; "Don't covet your neighbor's possessions"; "Don't burn down your neighbor's house"; "Don't falsify evaluation reports." Everyday social life depends on such agreements. In fact, there is an enormous amount of agreement on many value issues in contemporary societies, highly publicized disagreements notwithstanding. If there were not, these societies could not exist.

Alternatively, choosing "Grass is green" to illustrate the decidability of factual claims masks the disagreement that so often characterizes the cutting edge of science. In addition to the wave theory of light, we might consider the heliocentric theory of the solar system (in Galileo's time), the collision theory of the disappearance of the dinosaurs, the big bang theory, and so on. These were all hotly contested at one time.

Contributing further to the unbalanced diet of examples so as to encourage the perception of an epistemological divide between science and the values is the fact that scientific communities are relatively small and insulated, incorporate restricted ranges of interests, and have disagreements that are hidden from public view. By comparison, the moral-political community is huge, the interests it incorporates are vast, and the disagreements are open for all to see.

Yet another place where science and values converge is in the norms for science. Normative principles are as much a part of Campbell's (1982) "tools of descriptive science and logic" as they are of moral-political discourse. They specify *good* practice in terms of regulative values, just as they guide practice in evaluation. Compare "Violating the law of noncontradiction is irrational" and "Deliberately falsifying evaluation results is wrong." The point is that both rationality and science, as well as morality and politics, are regulated by substantive values.

A third reason that belief in the undecidability of values has persisted is the ocular model of knowledge—construing knowledge as a "mirror of nature" (Rorty, 1979). We can check to see whether grass is green just by looking. On the other hand, however unimpeachable the prohibition against torturing children may be, there is no way to check it to *see* if it mirrors the way things are, out there, in reality.

There is a difference here in what we can see and what we cannot, but we think that it marks a difference *within* the domain of knowledge rather than *between* knowledge and some pretender (value claims). For example, the common explanation for persons who persistently claim to see pink elephants is that they are irrational. The same serves as the explanation for persons who insist it is okay to torture children for fun. In this way at least, the two cases are epistemologically similar (see, e.g., Taylor, 1995).

We are not suggesting that *no* differences ever exist between fact and value claims, between science and politics, between descriptive valuing and prescriptive valuing. Rather, we are suggesting that the differences between them are much narrower than is often thought because they are less epistemologically different than most accounts suggest, as well as being confounded with each other. The differences are not fundamental enough to imply that evaluators cannot draw rational evaluative conclusions.

THE EMOTIVE CONCEPTION
OF DEMOCRACY

In this part of the chapter we investigate what conception of democracy seems logically consistent with the received view. We believe that all evaluators must have *some* broad conception of how their studies will inform society and, indeed, some conception of democracy and of evaluation's role in it, even if this conception is not made explicit. The received view seems consistent with what we call *emotive democracy* (a term inspired by MacIntyre, 1981) or *preferential democracy*. It may be the case that Shadish et al. hold some other view of which we are not aware, although emotive democracy seems consistent with their stated views.

In emotive democracy value claims are put forth by stakeholders and accepted at face value, as are preferences. A value is a value is a value, and value claims compete against one another in the public arena. The strength of this view is that it explains how American democracy seems to work currently. The weakness is that it seems to embrace the status quo.

Shadish et al. reject comprehensive theories of justice as unsuitable for evaluation because they are prescriptive and people disagree about them. However, emotive democracy is a "prescriptive theory" also, which is used to frame evaluation practice and criticize other evaluation theorists. The two roles it leaves for evaluators are means depiction and interest group depiction, both of which seem too restrictive to us.

Prescriptive Theories

Shadish et al. equate a "prescriptive theory" with a broad political theory, such as Rawls's (1971) theory of justice. They invoke the undecidability of values to show how employing prescriptive theories is to be avoided because it conflicts with fostering a "pluralism of values" (p. 456). They support their argument in two ways: (a) They say there are "credible alternatives" to Rawls's theory (p. 456)—that is, Nozick's (1974) theory in particular; and (b) they say that "justice is just one moral concern in evaluation, along with human rights, equality, liberty, and utility" (p. 456). Hence, because there is no way to decide between competing theories of justice or between justice and other values, evaluators should bracket values and confine themselves to "descriptive theory."

We don't think these are conclusive arguments. First, Shadish et al. write as if they were providing an *alternative to employing a prescriptive theory* when, in actuality, they are *employing an alterna-*

tive prescriptive theory of their own: Don't employ Rawls's and similar theories because that would violate fostering a pluralism of values. In this way, they are not agnostics because they implicitly reject Rawls's theory. They implicitly reject Nozick's as well.

Second, Rawls and Nozick do disagree, but disagreement does not imply that no one can be right. Despite rancorous disagreement, the Emancipation Proclamation and the decision in *Brown v. Board of Education* were correct. And because most people disagreed with Galileo, it did not follow that he could not be right about whether the earth revolves around the sun. Disagreement per se does not mean one side cannot be right or wrong.

Third, Rawls and Nozick offer comprehensive theories in terms of a complex constellation of concepts and principles, such as human rights, equality, liberty, and utility. An important aspect of such theories is that they distinguish and rank various "values." Rawls and Nozick offer liberal-egalitarian and libertarian accounts, and, although they disagree, especially regarding how to interpret equality and liberty, they both distinguish between what individuals have a right to and what they merely "value" (i.e., desire). For example, one person's right to nondiscrimination is different from another's desire to retire in Boca Raton. And should the two come into conflict, the right to nondiscrimination should take precedence over the desire for an extravagant retirement.

Shadish et al.'s view lumps all values together—justice, equality, rights, life, liberty, profits, needs of the disadvantaged, defense, health care, taxes. The undecidability of values thesis looms large here: Because values are discordant and on a par, there is no justification for engaging in joint deliberation about differences in values in order to find common ground. Democracy based on these premises is characterized by a scramble on the part of various interest groups to pursue their own interests.

The substance of competing values is irrelevant, because a value is a value is a value. To be democratic, evaluators should confine themselves to "descriptive valuing," to describing values relative to stakeholders' views and to treating these views the same way. To advance some views as more compelling than others is to engage in "prescriptive valuing." So the reasoning seems to go.

Consider the following passage, in which Shadish et al. criticize the idea that social programs should be evaluated in terms of how well they serve the needs of the disadvantaged:

> Many stakeholders in American social policy would dispute the assumptions and recommendations of needs-based theories of justice about redressing social inequities. . . the assumptions and recommendations of such egalitarian theories are probably not operational in U.S. social policy (Lindblom, 1977). When policy is being framed and implemented, participants in the policy process rarely seek to ensure that the needs of the most disadvantaged Americans are met before other needs. . . . Recent history suggests that policy may be shaped as much or more by defense policy, health care costs, taxes, and priorities that serve constituencies other than the disadvantaged. Selecting criteria of merit from needs-based theories of justice may result in evaluations that differ dramatically from the terms used in policy debates. This can minimize the usefulness of such evaluations. (pp. 96-97)

Despite some cautions—"probably not operational," "may result in," "can minimize"—the message is that the disadvantaged can make no special claims against other constituencies, say, *Fortune 500* CEOs, defense contractors, or wealthy investors. The claims of the disadvantaged ought to be treated on a par with others and then only if they employ the "terms used in policy debates."

This characterization may be accurate in its portrayal of how our political system functions and of the "terms of policy debates" it employs, but do we want to *prescribe* the status quo? Would we do the same in the antebellum South or pre-*Brown*? If so, we would still be committed to some kind of political framework that determines how society's goods ought to be distributed.

Means Depiction and
Interest Group Depiction

The received view sanctions two roles for evaluation at its intersection with the political system and policy making: means depiction and interest group depiction. Both are grounded in the undecidability of values and value minimalism. However, they differ in the extremes to which they take these as a consequence of how much (ungrounded) agreement they believe exists (or ought to exist) with respect to values.

Means depiction is the role for evaluation that Donald Campbell's theory assumes. The assumption is that although values (ends) evade justification in a way the facts (means) do not, there are nonetheless some ends that are or ought to be "accepted," such as ameliorating poverty. The role for evaluation is to investigate the means by which such ends might be realized, and then to inform policy makers.

Because it incorporates the undecidability of values, means depiction can foster social change only so long as the ends go largely unchallenged. When agreement breaks down, no cognitive resources are available with which to argue that ends, such as the elimination of poverty, should be placed in front of other ends, such as boosting skier visits to Aspen.

Another problem with means depiction is that it is better suited to a technocratic society than to a democratic one (Fay, 1975; Howe, 1992). This is true whether means depiction is working smoothly or not. Means, after all, are means only relative to some end. Adopting a given end—say, increased computer literacy—entails focusing evaluation on the limited array of means that may be used to accomplish this end. Consequently, such an investigation of means presupposes the value orientation of those who support this end from among many others who might compete for resources.

Interest group depiction is associated with newer versions of the received view. Rather than investigating grand means to grand ends for the entire society, the role for evaluation is to construct "value summaries" for the stakeholders: "If X is important to you, then evaluand Y is good for the following reasons" (Shadish et al., 1995, p. 101). Evaluation confines itself to making conditional statements to policy makers.

Isn't this democracy? Isn't democracy about giving everyone an equal voice? Yes. Isn't it about not having one group impose its view of the good life on others? Yes. And doesn't interest group depiction facilitate just these things? Well, no—because certain background conditions required of democracy are not met. It is not the case that disadvantaged groups are able to have their interests represented equally with those of others in politics and policy making. Left to their own devices, there is no way the disadvantaged can have equal voice. The disadvantaged are subject to having other people's views of the good life imposed on them.

One remedy is to have evaluators seek out the needs of the disadvantaged. But this remedy is blocked by Shadish et al. in their version of the received view. Such a practice is to be avoided because it can "minimize the usefulness" of evaluations by couching them in a vocabulary not used in policy debates. Furthermore, bringing the needs of the disadvantaged to the table violates the prohibition on prescriptive valuing by presupposing a needs-based theory of justice. In our view, eschewing needs-based reasoning thwarts democratic deliberation by fortifying the power status quo.

Apparently, Shadish et al. would include the *interests* (versus *needs*) of the disadvantaged under the right conditions: if (a) this does not violate the vocabulary of policy making and (b) the interests of the disadvantaged receive no special treatment—that is, are treated as just one among other "value summaries." Shadish et al. add this condition: (c) The disadvantaged should speak for themselves rather than have others speak for them; this is required in order to stay within the confines of descriptive valuing.

Thus, when evaluators clear the necessary hurdles placed in front of them regarding when it is legitimate to seek out and include the interests of the disadvantaged and how those interests must be weighed, they are admonished to make sure the disadvantaged speak for themselves. Again, this is required for evaluators to stay within the confines of descriptive valuing: "Having the disadvantaged speak for themselves is descriptive valuing" (Shadish et al., 1995, p. 51).

Does this mean that evaluators should be scribes, writing down what various stakeholders hold and then presenting their "value summaries" to policy makers? Or should evaluators provide relevant information, to prompt, probe, edit, translate, seek clarifications, and recast? The latter actions shade into prescriptive valuing on the part of evaluators, and it is difficult (impossible?) to avoid these sorts of actions in representing people's views, even in their own voices.

The admonition to have the disadvantaged speak for themselves assumes that whoever describes the perspective of the disadvantaged affects the prescriptive valuing that description contains. And what does this mean if not that descriptive valuing and prescriptive valuing cannot be disentangled, that, save being mere scribes, evaluators can't do one without doing the other? Otherwise, evaluators could represent anyone's views and interests with no danger of falling into prescriptive valuing.

It is clear that the disadvantaged, through no fault of their own, are often not in a good position to speak for themselves—they may lack information, time, transportation, and political savvy, and can be mistrustful and intimidated. In short, they lack access. True enough, there are dangers in deciding what is best for groups from a distance, misguided paternalism being one (though attributing to everyone a desire for adequate food, shelter, health care, and education seems fairly safe). We deal with this issue later by making dialogue a critical component of evaluation.

In conclusion, many evaluators accept some version of the view that facts and values are two distinct things and must be kept separate in theory and practice. Such a conception is counter to the best thinking in philosophy and may lead to less-than-ideal practices. It may place evaluators in the position of serving whatever interests the clients or policy makers have and supporting the status quo distribution of power.

By contrast, we assert that both facts and values can be subjected to rational argument in the context of evaluation studies. Evidence can be collected for and against the validity of such evaluative statements and their truth debated. No goals or values are out of bounds for inspection. This provides evaluators with a broader role vis-à-vis society. In assuming such a role, however, evaluators should proceed from explicitly justified professional frameworks.

THE RADICAL
CONSTRUCTIVIST VIEW

—————•◆•—————

his chapter begins an examination of *dialogical* approaches to evaluation. A dialogical view is one based on the central premise that evaluation and social research must proceed by engaging research subjects—participants—in dialogue. In fact, our own deliberative democratic view is dialogical as well and shares important features with other such views.

In this and the next chapter we explicate two dialogical views that should be distinguished from the deliberative democratic view: radical constructivism (represented by Guba and Lincoln) and postmodernism (represented by Stronach and MacLure). Again we have chosen leading theorists in these areas to critique, and we hasten to recognize their important overall contributions to the field. We want to examine their underlying premises about values and how these affect their theory and practice.

Dialogical view refers to the general methodological approach spawned by the "interpretive turn" in social research (Rabinow & Sullivan, 1979). Interpretivism is the philosophy of social science, now in ascendancy, that gained prominence in the mid-20th century. Its hallmark feature is the conception of social life and social knowledge as contingent on the existence of human beings, their activities, and how they interpret and construct the social world. Values are to be found in the interstices of these activities, interpretations, and constructions, and values are uncovered—as well as created—through dialogue. They are not just "out there" (or "in there") waiting to be cataloged. Dialogue is critical.

In general, interpretivism rejects the view that a pristine scientific language—a language for describing things neutrally among theories and values—can be devised and used to characterize and interpret human behavior (a tenet of positivism). There is no chance that researchers may escape their contingent and self-referential predicament and attain a wholly detached perspective. As Charles Taylor (1987) puts it, "We have to think of man as a self-interpreting animal. . . . There is no such thing as the structure of meanings for him independently of his interpretation of them" (p. 46).

Exactly how the fact-value distinction is worked out divides interpretivists. The positivists associated facts with science, means, cognition, objectivity, truth, and rationality. On the value side were politics, ends, interests, subjectivity, power, and irrationality. By contrast, "radical constructivists" deny a sharp fact-value distinction by applying the radical undecidability thesis (reserved for values in the received view) to *both* sides of the fact-value distinction. There is no truth or objectivity to be found anywhere.

Our own view denies a sharp fact-value distinction by applying the radical undecidability thesis to *neither* side of the fact-value distinction. Although science and truth can be corrupted—"distorted"— by underlying values, interests, and power, truth claims are nonetheless subject to rational examination and are redeemable if generated in a way consistent with the procedural requirements of impartiality so as to prevent self-serving values, interests, and power from dominating.

RADICAL CONSTRUCTIVISM CHARACTERIZED

The foremost theorists of radical constructivist evaluation are Guba and Lincoln (1989), who deny the existence of any objective reality. In their view, "reality" is completely a human construction that depends entirely on agreement among participants: "Now constructions are, quite literally, created realities. They do not exist outside the persons who create and hold them; they are not part of some 'objective' world that exists apart from their constructors" (p. 143). Even cause-and-effect relations are merely "mental imputations" and not "real" in any empirical sense.

Given that there are as many constructed "social realities" as there are individuals, the purpose of an evaluation is to negotiate a common understanding among these multiple realities, which can then be used as a basis for action. "Truth" is a matter of consensus among individuals and groups and has no meaning beyond that, in Guba and Lincoln's view. Their model for evaluation is the "hermeneutic dialectic circle" of inquiry.

In their approach to evaluation, the major stakeholders are first identified and their concerns, beliefs, and so on are carefully solicited. Second, all stakeholder views are submitted to other stakeholders for comments and criticism. Third, those issues that have not been resolved by this initial discussion become the advance organizers for data collected by evaluators in the next stage of the evaluation. Finally, this collected information is considered by all stakeholders in a joint discussion, and there is an attempt to reach consensus on each disputed item.

Findings are arrived at by joint construction when elected representatives of the various groups negotiate with each other. Participants go around in circles, revealing their own views of the situation and challenging others. Consensus is attained through each group's confronting other groups and better understanding its own position and those of other groups. In fact, sets of fundamental beliefs (paradigms) cannot be proved or disproved, according to this view. They are what people accept as basic. The only thing that can be done is to encourage participants to open up to other viewpoints and contribute to a joint consensus.

The process ends when consensus is reached or time and resources run out. Some items will be agreed on, some partially agreed on, and some not agreed on at all. However, resolution of issues implies action. "By their joint agreement they commit themselves jointly to accept continuing responsibility and accountability for whatever action is taken" (Guba & Lincoln, 1989, pp. 222-223). During this process evaluators assume the roles of mediator, facilitator, collaborator, learner, teacher, "reality shaper," and change agent. "Evaluators are orchestrators of a negotiation process that aims to culminate in consensus on better informed and more sophisticated constructions" (p. 110).

Evaluators insert their own opinions only later in the dialectic process and even then place their views alongside others for consideration. Bringing evaluator views in too early would result in too much weight being given to them. Evaluator constructions should not be privileged over others, except by reason of superior information or more sophistication. In Guba and Lincoln's view, the chance that evaluator biases will shape the conclusions is low, provided the process is conducted in accordance with hermeneutic dialectical principles.

However, it is possible for these constructions to be wrong. "Malconstructions" can be incomplete, simplistic, uninformed, internally inconsistent, or derived through inadequate methodology. Constructions can be challenged by new information and increased sophistication in dealing with information. "Understanding that the only viable alternative to relativism is absolutism, and that absolutism is not a position congruent with the American democratic ideal, those stakeholders may suddenly become much more open to alternatives" (Guba & Lincoln, 1989, p. 218).

Although there are many things to admire in Guba and Lincoln's involvement of stakeholders, their view runs into serious difficulties. The existence of an outside empirical reality of some kind is easily demonstrated. Even if everyone in the room agrees that you can put your hand through a table, you cannot put your hand through a table. There is little disagreement among leading philosophers about the existence of such a reality, though there are disputes about the nature of social reality and its relationship to thinking and actions.

Involving stakeholders in evaluations is worthy, in our view, but how can their ideas and concerns be used? Do all views count equally? What is the basis on which stakeholders argue with one another? Ordinarily, we would think that facts would make a difference. But if there is no reality, no facts to appeal to, why should we attend to data collected by the evaluator? What difference does it make? We believe what we believe, and data from a nonexistent reality can hardly count.

> We would simply stress again that the question, "But which view is right?" is inappropriate. Views are neither right nor wrong but different depending on how the construction is formed, the context in which it is formed, and the values that undergird construction in the first place. It is not more research that is needed but more negotiation. (Guba & Lincoln, 1989, p. 255)

Guba and Lincoln cite inconsistency as an error. But what difference would inconsistency make? If we hold views and they have nothing to do with any outside reality or are inconsistent with one another, so what? Guba and Lincoln make frequent reference to "sophisticated" beliefs being better, or better-informed beliefs being better. However, if all views are equal and not connected to reality, why would these be better?

The point is that such criteria presume something outside the beliefs themselves and a commitment that consistency or sophistication or more information will lead to a better construction. A new view can be better only in reference to something outside the beliefs. So there is some inconsistency with the subjective views held by participants and the intersubjective norms required to reach agreement.

We also question Guba and Lincoln's position on moral grounds. Suppose that a participant advances a racist view. Are we to hold that this view is as good as other views? It is no use arguing that other stakeholders would disagree. Others may have disagreed in the past without changing the person's attitude. Do we have no way as evaluators of saying anything is wrong with a racist view? If not, then evaluation has no way of condemning even morally reprehensible beliefs. To say that we can have no way of resisting these views suggests why relativism is untenable. (Of course, we don't think Guba and Lincoln personally would tolerate these views in their own work. They would find ways of confronting such ideas, but we doubt that their methods for doing so would be consistent with relativist principles.)

Although stakeholder participation is highly desirable, equality of beliefs cannot be an ultimate guiding principle for evaluations. Rather, some viewpoints will be better than others—some will be factually incorrect and some will be morally wrong. Even in relativist constructions, people must challenge each other if justifiable value judgments are to result.

There is a sense in which findings are relative to their particular setting and context in that they are socially produced in a time and place by particular people speaking a particular language. Findings are not infallible and are subject to challenge by others who can raise proper criticisms. This sense of (sociological) relativism is true. However, there is another thesis that asserts that all beliefs are equally valid, and that there are no rational grounds for preferring one over another. This (judgmental) relativism is false.

Often relativists think that because knowledge is socially produced it cannot be criticized rationally, but the second thesis does not
follow from the first. In fact, the criteria for choosing one position
over another require that one position is better informed, more
consistent, more coherent, more rational, or morally superior in some
way. The fact that findings are socially produced does not mean they
cannot be true or false.

Having pointed to these general flaws, we turn now to a closer
philosophical examination of radical constructivist views.

FACTS, VALUES, AND EPISTEMOLOGY

Guba and Lincoln claim that positivism is not wrong or untrue but
is "ill-informed and unsophisticated." Why do they do make such a
claim?

> The relativist constructivist, while not agreeing with the
> positivist formulation, can nonetheless accept it as one of
> many constructions. The constructivist may find the positiv-
> ist view ill-informed and unsophisticated, but not *wrong* or
> *untrue*. (Guba & Lincoln, 1989, p. 16)

There is an epistemological tension within Guba and Lincoln's
"relativist constructivist" approach. On the one hand, they hold that
all beliefs, claims, theories, and values are "constructions" embedded
in human existence. Moreover, they are extreme—"radical"—in their
view, for "constructions" are highly *subjective*, idiosyncratic things,
created by individual "constructors" and relative to particular points
of view.

On the other hand, they do not shrink from advocating and
making judgments that are *intersubjective*, for example, regarding the
merit of social programs and theories such as positivism. But war-
ranted intersubjective judgments (e.g., "The earth revolves around

the sun"; "Torturing children for the sheer fun of it is wrong") rule out individual subjective "constructions" that disagree, or so it would seem.

To avoid this inconsistency, Guba and Lincoln opt for evaluating "constructions" intersubjectively in terms of whether they are sophisticated and well-informed rather than in terms of whether they are right and true. What makes a view sophisticated and well-informed? Proper attention to evidence. What makes a view right and true? Again, proper attention to evidence. Thus, they employ "sophisticated" or "unsophisticated" and "well-informed" or "ill-informed" as surrogates for right or wrong and true or false. If they didn't employ such surrogates and there were no criteria to decide, there would be no reason to prefer their "constructions" over others, including those of positivism (or the "conventional paradigm," as they call it; p. 83).

In their minds they are providing a constructivist alternative to the "conventional paradigm." Two things seem to be central in their reasoning: (a) Key epistemological concepts like truth must be jettisoned by virtue of certain interpretations that have been attached to them; for instance, that "p is true" = "p is certain and universally so." Yet on the other hand, (b) jettisoning truth (and the "absolutism" with which it is associated) as the guiding criterion need not result in one's embracing the extreme view that "anything goes" (p. 256). So, according to this reasoning, truth must be jettisoned because of the first point and new criteria must be introduced to take its place because of the second.

This line of reasoning makes sense only if truth is interpreted as universal and certain. But such an interpretation is closer to Plato than to positivism. It is only on the basis of a rather dubious characterization of positivism that we can find support for rejecting the concept of truth altogether. Here we rehearse some history in the philosophy of science. We begin with positivism, move to the Kuhnian alternative, and then to the interpretive turn in social science to show how the demise of positivism need not lead to radical constructivism.

Contrary to Guba and Lincoln's interpretation, the positivists had a markedly falliblist bent toward truth. Indeed, the only truths that could count as certain and universal (a priori) in their view were so-called analytic truths that amounted to little more than conventions of logic; for example, "If p, then p," or of word meanings, such as "All bachelors are unmarried." Other candidates for truth were subject to the requirement of verification (or falsification) in terms of specifiable observation consequences, and such truths were always fallible, always subject to being overturned by new observational evidence.

Also, the positivists were *not* realists—a common confusion. The idea that there could be any *really* real things, distinct from what could be reduced to observation consequences, was anathema for them, so much metaphysical nonsense, some of them thought (e.g., Ayer, 1936). In fact, the behaviorists, inspired by positivism, took this stance toward thoughts, minds, and souls—so much metaphysics to be eliminated in favor of observables.

Rather, positivists were *objectivists* of an extreme kind, rather than realists. They held not that there existed really real things "out there," but that the contents of observation could be (and should be) wholly neutral and intersubjective. (Their failure to work out this thesis in a satisfactory way was an ongoing source of embarrassment for positivists—among other things, it was a metaphysical thesis itself!)

Finally, and here Guba and Lincoln are certainly on the right track, the positivists eliminated values from the domain of truth and science. Like metaphysical claims, value claims could not measure up to the requirements of verification: Value claims, such as "Abortion is morally acceptable," are not analytically true or false, nor can the observation consequences that would render them empirically true or false be specified. For this reason the positivists embraced the "radical undecidability thesis" of values—values cannot be decided rationally. For positivists, there was nothing to render value claims true or false because, as in metaphysics, there was (literally) nothing to be right or wrong about.

Now, the positivists were criticized from many directions, but the most devastating criticisms were aimed at the verifiability principle (see, e.g., Howe, 1985, 1988; Phillips, 1983). This principle may be stated as follows: Any claim that is to qualify as "cognitively significant," as capable of truth or falsity, must be either *analytic* (true or false in virtue of logic or meaning) or *synthetic* (true or false in virtue of observation consequences). The aim was to zero in on genuine science and eliminate metaphysics as well as self-serving, biased values.

But the verifiability principle itself proved untenable. Positivists were never able to provide a satisfactory account of it, and there was significant disagreement within positivist ranks. Finally, Quine (1962, chap. 2) and Kuhn (1962) launched a critique from outside that successfully challenged the root assumption: that the purely empirical (observational) may be separated from the purely conceptual (theoretical). The alternative picture provided by Quine and Kuhn is that all observation is "theory-laden"; all observation is relative to a "conceptual scheme" or "paradigm." Thus, there can be no scientific claims that are neutral and objective in the sense that they do not presuppose a conceptual scheme or paradigm.

However, Quine and Kuhn did *not* draw the conclusion from the insight that observation is theory-laden that we ought to throw out truth along with positivism, that knowledge is *merely* interpretation. Rather, truth—as well as objectivity and rationality—must be reinterpreted (reconstructed) in more defensible ways. So they did not embrace radical relativism.

To be sure, the Quinean-Kuhnian account introduces a form of relativity of knowledge, namely, relativity to conceptual schemes. It is also "constructivist" in the sense that knowledge cannot be abstracted from human activity and human conceptualizing. But this kind of relativism-cum-constructivism is a far cry from radical, individualistic constructivism. There remains room for truth, objectivity, and rationality within communities that share conceptual schemes because such communities inherently incorporate standards that serve as the basis for their identities and for intersubjective judgments among their members. Indeed, one of Kuhn's major points is the social and socializing character of scientific paradigms.

Furthermore, although moves from one conceptual scheme to another cannot be characterized in terms of mechanical rules and are not straightforwardly cumulative, such scientific "revolutions," or "paradigm shifts," as Kuhn calls them, are not based on subjective and arbitrary beliefs, either. Shared problems, vocabulary, and methodological canons specific to a given area of scientific endeavor loom large in dealing with anomalous findings. Even where a scientific "revolution" is on the horizon, the old paradigm overlaps significantly with the new one, even if it is not straightforwardly subsumable (the positivist account of scientific progress) (Kuhn, 1977).

In general, overarching "values" (as Kuhn calls them) or "pragmatic criteria" (as Quine calls them) apply intersubjectively so as to circumscribe what theories ("constructions") are viable candidates and to determine which among them wins out. Among these values or criteria are consistency, coherence, scope, simplicity, and explanatory power (Kuhn, 1977; Quine, 1970).

Again, the Quinean-Kuhnian alternative to positivism does not jettison truth, scientific rationality, and objectivity. It reinterprets these concepts in a way that dispenses with the pristine observational basis for science associated with positivism's verifiability principle and brings them into line with the history of theoretical advances. Rationality, objectivity, and truth seeking remain hallmarks of the scientific enterprise, and these are intersubjective concepts. They constrain claims and conjectures that individual "constructors" devise. In contrast to the radical, individualistic version, "constructivism" is an irremediably social act performed with irremediably social materials.

We draw several conclusions from this. First, intersubjective criteria are required to head off the specter of "anything goes." The general strategy of postpositivist thinkers has been to reinterpret rather than jettison truth and related concepts. Another reason not to abandon truth, objectivity, and rationality for less familiar notions, such as sophistication and well-informedness, is the circumlocution.

For example, is the claim "George Washington was the first president of the United States" true? Is it well-informed and sophisticated? What's the difference? Both respond to evidence, presumably.

Second, a corollary requirement of intersubjective criteria is that true/false and right/wrong will exist *and* some "constructors" may be in a better position to decide what is what. That is, experts exist who have authority over nonexperts in given arenas of knowledge. What gives them this authority is their immersion in a particular literature, familiarity with a given problematic and the vocabulary in which it is couched, and mastery of the acceptable means of seeking truth. For us, this means that evaluators have special expertise based on training and experience that others do not have. Their abilities should be put to good use.

Third, scientific controversies are decidable in principle. This does not mean that accepted theories are infallible. Nor does it mean that scientific controversies are decidable only by appeal to criteria that may be mechanically applied to neutral observations that serve as inert building blocks of knowledge (which positivists did believe; Howe, 1985, 1988).

However, matters are messier as we move from natural science to social science and evaluation: First, the verifiability principle is doubly problematic in social research, for social reality is a two-way construction, such that its "objects" (subjects, participants), unlike the objects in physics, themselves interpret and are governed by norms. Put another way, their observations are also *theory-laden* and must be treated as such. Thus, social reality should be investigated dialogically. Certainly Guba and Lincoln would agree with this emphatically.

Second, among the norms that are interpreted by research participants and that govern their behavior are moral and political values, such that values are implicit in the vocabulary of social research in a way they are not in natural science (Howe, 1985, 1988; Rorty, 1982; Scriven, 1969)—compare "racism" with "velocity," for instance. The crucial question is how these values are to be unearthed and negotiated in the conduct of evaluation.

This process may take different forms. Ironically, the radical constructivist view embraces a view of values that shares some important features with the positivist view. As a corollary of the verifiability principle, the positivists developed an "emotivist" theory of values. Because claims about values are not claims that can be "cognitively significant," cognitive concepts such as justification, argument, and reasoning do not apply to values. Value claims are individual expressions of emotions, in their view. Despite surface appearances, the cognitive status of "Abortion is wrong" is much more on a par with "Boo abortion!" than with "Grass is green."

This does not mean that individuals cannot win approval from others for their value stance, but the basic mechanism is *causal* rather than *justificatory*. Suppose, for instance, that someone opposes abortion and is trying to convince those who approve of it to change their minds. In an effort to stir their emotions, the advocate might show them pictures of fetuses, videotapes of abortions, and so on. The objective is not to get them to *embrace the proposition* "Abortion is wrong," but to *create in them the negative emotions* toward abortion that "Abortion is wrong," when uttered, expresses. We might even invoke reason in the effort to do this by saying, "If you're against murder, you must be against abortion."

However, reason functions only indirectly to bring the underlying emotions into line, in this view. Claims that abortion counts as murder have force only to the extent that they exploit preexisting (and noncognitive) negative attitudes toward murder. Thus, reasoning about values takes hypothetical form: "*If* you embrace value X, then you must also embrace value Y."

Consider now Guba and Lincoln's (1989) characterization of their "constructivist" (or "naturalist") view:

> Social reality is not objectively "out there," but exists only as
> a series of mental and social constructions derived via social
> interactions. Rather than looking for an external reality the
> naturalist looks for internal realities—the sense-making and

belief structures that order human existence and exist only
within individuals. It is the holders of those realities . . . who
provide whatever warrant exists. The warrant is thus no more
powerful or pervasive than are the persons who hold the
constructions. (p. 137)

They continue:

The primacy of verification procedures is eliminated since
there is nothing to verify. The object of naturalistic inquiry
is to identify and describe various *emic* constructions and
place those constructions in touch—with the intent of evolving a more informed and sophisticated construction than any
single one of the emic constructions, *or* the researcher's or
evaluator's *etic* construction, represents. (p. 138)

And finally:

The naturalistic approach does not seek justification of anyone's present position but rather seeks *connection* between
positions as a means to move to higher intellectual, moral,
and ethical ground. (p. 140)

Guba and Lincoln give no indication in these passages that they
endorse the emotivist account of the *meaning* of value claims as
disguised expressions of emotions. To the contrary, their use of such
terms as *constructions* and *belief-structures* indicates that they hold
a different view. But emotivism also had a particular stance toward
the *justification* of value claims—the undecidability of values thesis.
And we may forgo the emotivist analysis of meaning and yet retain
its stance toward justification (MacIntyre, 1981), which Guba and
Lincoln appear to do.

They share three features with emotivist justification. First, value
claims are subjective and express only what is "within individuals."

Second, warrant is identified with the power and persuasiveness of individuals promoting value claims. No further criteria exist "out there" against which to measure the warrant or to "verify" value claims intersubjectively. Third, following from the first two, removing disagreements in values should not be approached as attempts to arrive at the right (true, most justified) position to which people *should* agree. Rather, removing such disagreements should be approached as attempts to align beliefs, constructions, emotions—to forge "connections"—to which people *will* agree.

In this way Guba and Lincoln's conception of the epistemological status of values is similar to the received view's conception in accepting the undecidability of values. Guba and Lincoln differ by not drawing a sharp line between facts and values and by not applying radical undecidability only to the latter. As radical constructivists, they apply undecidability across the board to all truth claims and disagreements. Thus, it is their general epistemological view, radical constructivism, not only their view of the epistemological status of values, that distinguishes their view from the received view. And this undergirds how they approach the practice of evaluation.

THE PRACTICE OF EVALUATION

Guba and Lincoln (1989) advocate a "hermeneutic dialectic process" for evaluation (p. 149). This is a dialogical approach, but it has one important peculiarity: *hyper-egalitarianism*. Not only are all affected stakeholders to be heard (or represented), the mark of dialogical approaches in general, but no knowledge claims ("constructions") whatsoever, including the evaluator's, are to be given any privileged position relative to other knowledge claims, however expertly and rigorously such claims might have been derived and supported. Evaluators are to assume the role of "mediator and facilitator" in this process.

This raises the question of whether there is any place for the expert knowledge and skills of evaluators qua evaluators. If evaluators are to be anything but mediators, shouldn't they know and be able to introduce pertinent social research findings as well as their own "constructions," presumably the result of the competent application of empirical research methods, into the process? Guba and Lincoln answer this challenge with respect to social research findings in the following way:

> Documentary data, literature analects, or the inquirer's own construction may seem, to respondents, to be beyond reproach. . . . We recommend, therefore, that such external materials be introduced in a way that does not reveal their source. Instead of saying, for example, "Census bureau documents show . . ." or "The literature on learning shows that . . ." or "It is my own opinion, based on years of research that . . . ," one might simply introduce any proposition by saying, "Some people believe that . . ." or "It is sometimes said that . . ." and invite comment. (p. 154)

Later, they say:

> Parallel to the case of professional literature, we think that the evaluator's construction would be invested with too much weight if announced to be that. However, if the evaluator's construction is introduced again in some low-key way—"Some people believe that . . ."—it is open to critique without fear of reprisal or embarrassment. (p. 213)

To avoid the technocratic excesses of positivism, radical constructivism journeys too far in the other direction, with paradoxical results, in our view. First, like the received view, Guba and Lincoln prescribe that evaluators should not prescribe. If this were a merely *strategic* principle, it would be worth heeding; for example, "You won't get very far if you ignore people's views and assert your authority." But there should still be somewhere to get to—for example, more equal social arrangements. Whether, when, and to what degree to invoke the strategic principle would be an empirical question.

But they go farther than this. For Guba and Lincoln, this principle is *epistemological*. For them, there is nothing to "verify," no "out there," nothing to be "right or wrong" about, so we get the principle, "No one ought to advance his or her view as the correct one." The paradox is that, if true, this principle defeats itself, for it is not something we can be right or wrong about. This leads to paralysis: Evaluators should not advance their views as correct. But what if some others advance theirs as correct? To be consistent, should evaluators refrain from advancing their view that others should not advance theirs as correct?

Second, Guba and Lincoln advocate a "hands-off" approach to the question of values. Apparently, participants are unable to evaluate critically anything the evaluator might say (such claims must be disguised as "Some people believe . . ."). Now, we would argue that more credence should be put in what the Census Bureau has concluded about the number of homeless than in, say, what a man or woman on the street has concluded. The paradox here is that this position seems to neither empower nor protect the public.

Certainly, power is an important issue. But hyper-egalitarianism has as much potential to exacerbate as to reduce power imbalances in evaluation. The means offered for equalizing power is to check the authority of evaluators. But evaluators are not uniformly authoritarian or biased. Furthermore, they are by no means the only ones who wield power. The biggest threats might well come from other stakeholders, clients, and sponsors (Chelimsky, 1998). Limiting evaluators to the roles of mere facilitators and mediators gives free rein to *these* sources of power.

Guba and Lincoln do anticipate this problem. One of the things they require is a "willingness on the part of all parties to *share power*" (p. 150). But this won't address the problem if all it means is that everyone is heard by a facilitator. And if this is supposed to acknowledge the need for special protections for disadvantaged stakeholders within an evaluation, it requires something radical constructivism

cannot embrace. For instance, certain social research findings, constructions, knowledge claims, whatever, are right, true, have warrant
in asserting that certain stakeholders are indeed disadvantaged. In
short, it requires that evaluators commit to the view that some
"constructions" of these matters are right and should guide evaluation practice, and other constructions are wrong and should be
dismissed.

In conclusion, if all Guba and Lincoln have in mind by "constructivism" is opening up evaluation to excluded voices, ensuring that
they are given their due, and supplanting concepts like "true" and
"right" with concepts like "sophisticated" and "well informed," then
we agree with them and their view is not far from the one we advance,
except for the shuffle in vocabulary.

But they appear to be advocating something more far-reaching
than replacing "true" and "false" with equivalent concepts. They
appear to embrace the undecidability of values thesis, which averts
moral-political commitment in the practice of evaluation. If so,
"constructivism" is seriously handicapped in fostering progressive
social change. Indeed, radical constructivism may be less able than
some advocates of the received view who "accept" and act on progressive values, even though they deny that such values can be
"justified."

We believe that evaluators should use their expertise by introduc-
ing authoritative evidence, even while we agree that dialogue is crucial
to evaluations. Evaluators should be more than facilitators, and they
should aspire to arrive at the truth, tentative as their claims may be.
These claims do not exist simply in participants' heads but in reality
itself, even though knowledge is not universal or absolute but is
context-bound and contingent.

5

THE POSTMODERNIST VIEW

———•◆•———

ostmodernism is much in vogue around the world, and there are so many versions that it is difficult to specify one definitive position. Relatively few people have written about postmodernism in evaluation or have tried to conduct postmodernist studies, though many admit to postmodern influences (Constas, 1998; Mabry, 1997; Stronach & MacLure, 1997). In social and educational research, there are many more adherents. Again, we take as exemplars of the postmodern view those who have taken these ideas farthest in evaluation, to our knowledge. Even though postmodernism is only emergent in evaluation, it is an intellectual force to be reckoned with.

Postmodernism takes the interpretive turn in a radical direction. In this view, the political philosophies and epistemologies dominant since the Enlightenment are at a dead end. The "emancipatory" project of modernity has exhausted itself. Reason will not solve our problems—quite the contrary. The task now is to "deconstruct," "denormalize," and "dismantle" the intellectual discourses we have developed. Grand projects that aspire to emancipate humanity are particularly suspicious. Liberal democracy and Marxism "terrorize" and marginalize people, in the postmodern view.

Whatever its merits as a form of skeptical philosophy, and however it is characterized (or itself "deconstructed"), postmodernism faces serious difficulties when applied to goal-oriented activities such as evaluation. The question of what follows "deconstruction" is often dismissed by postmodernists, if not greeted with hostility. Because postmodernism also applies the "radical undecidability thesis" to both sides of the fact-value distinction, it shares much with radical constructivism.

It differs with radical constructivism in important respects as well. Postmodernists are more insurgent than radical constructivists. They see themselves as intellectual provocateurs. They do not see insider perspectives as unproblematic. Insiders can be totally wrong in their ideas, misled by the social constructions in which they are enmeshed. Postmodernists see social life as shrouded in a contingent set of beliefs, values, and social arrangements that need to be problematized, deconstructed, and disrupted. And the job of evaluators is to do just that.

The (apparent) motivation of postmodernists is the liberation of humans from the taken-for-granted but ungrounded beliefs, values, social norms, and social practices that oppress them. In the end, their embrace of radical relativism condemns postmodernists to suffer moral-political inaction, or at least to have no articulated justifications for action, in our view. Otherwise, if they do commit to moral-political principles to guide and evaluate practice, they can be (and are) charged with being inconsistent, although they might well counter with characteristic irony that intellectual inconsistency does not impede action. In this chapter we outline the postmodernist view and show how some have applied it to evaluation.

FACTS, VALUES, AND EPISTEMOLOGY

Advocates of dialogical methods such as postmodernists share an interpretivist-constructivist epistemology, generally construed. That is, against classical empiricists and their offspring, the positivists, they uniformly reject what Dewey calls the "spectator view" of knowledge—the view that knowledge is built up piece by piece, by accumulation of an ever-growing and increasingly complex arrangement of passively received observations.

Instead, knowledge, particularly in social research, must be seen as actively constructed—as culturally and historically grounded, as laden with moral and political values, and as serving certain interests and purposes. So in this view facts and values are melded together. But this melding creates a formidable problem: Is knowledge (or what passes for it) *merely* a cultural-historical artifact? Is it *merely* a collection of moral and political values? Does it *merely* serve certain interests and purposes?

Postmodernists seem to answer yes to these questions—or at least to have no grounds for answering no. Lyotard (1987) notes, "I define *postmodern* as incredulity toward metanarratives" (p. 74). A metanarrative is a grand legitimating story, one important feature of which is its abstraction from time, place, and culture. Metanarratives include grand epistemological stories, such as the inevitable progress of science, and grand political stories, such as Marxism and liberalism. Postmodernists are highly skeptical about such stories because the narratives reinforce the regimes in power, in their view. Those in power construct such narratives and induce others to believe them. Indeed, that is a major reason they are in power. If not grand interpretative narratives, what then? Here is Lyotard's answer:

> The society of the future falls less within the province of a Newtonian anthropology . . . than a pragmatics of language particles. There are many language games—a heterogeneity

of elements. They only give rise to institutions in patches—
local determinism. . . . Is consensus to be obtained through
discussion . . . ? Such consensus does violence to the hetero-
geneity of language games. And invention is born of dissen-
sion. (pp. xxiv-xxv)

Michel Foucault (1987) shares Lyotard's skeptical attitude toward metanarratives and would supplant them with what he calls
"genealogy." Foucault's method is to trace the historical antecedents
that have given rise to the rationalization of modern institutions,
such as prisons and mental hospitals. For him, rationality is irremediably contingent. Institutions develop in specific historical circumstances and generate their own rationality, one that serves those in
power. In his view there can be no extrahistorical touchstones—
metanarratives—of the kind philosophers have sought since Plato.
    Related to this, knowledge and power are inextricably wedded in
"regimes of truth" that function to "normalize" persons—that is, to
render them acquiescent and "useful" vis-à-vis the institutions of
modern society, such as prisons, mental hospitals, and schools. Most
often, people are unconscious and unwitting victims of these regimes
of truth. Their own thinking imprisons them into accepting social
arrangements that may be contrary to their own interests, and they
are not aware of this.
    Hence, asking them to pool their own constructions of reality, as
in constructivist evaluations, can result in a pooling of ignorance, in
the postmodern view. Participants may merely reinforce each other's
ignorance, leading to even more mistaken views of the social regime
they are victimized by. And evaluations consistent with the received
view are likely to reinforce the concepts and regimes of truth that
those in power endorse. The effect of such evaluations is to "normalize" participants into accepting the dominant social structure. After
all, those in power sponsor and serve as audiences for evaluations.
Evaluation plays a strong legitimating role in society. Why else would
those in power fund it?

The question (overt or covert) now asked by the professional student, the State, or institutions of higher education is no longer, "Is it true?" but "What use is it?" In the context of the mercantilization of knowledge, more often than not this question is equivalent to: "Is it saleable?" And in the context of power-growth: "Is it efficient?" Having competence in a performance-oriented skill does indeed seem saleable. . . . What no longer makes the grade is competence as defined by other criteria—true/false, just/unjust, etc.—and, of course, low performativity in general. (Lyotard, 1984, p. 51)

Not only are facts and values intertwined, the operant values are those of the power regime and facts are shaped to fit them. Furthermore, these values often are inimical to the interests of most people in society. From the postmodernist view, what is needed are evaluation studies that alert people to their own predicament, studies that deconstruct or disrupt the normalizing influence of the truth regimes of the powerful.

In order to accomplish deconstruction and disruption in evaluations, Stronach and MacLure (1997) have advocated the use of survey questionnaires that take respondents out of the typical passive information provider role and make them both participants and judges of the conclusions of the study. Another tactic is for the evaluator to refuse to provide a metanarrative of the type that audiences of evaluation reports expect. Instead, a study might provide multiple competing narratives of events.

THE PRACTICE OF EVALUATION

Postmodernism has not made the same inroads into evaluation as it has in the humanities and social research. This makes sense, for how can we defend the practice of evaluation when the major thrust of postmodernism is to deny that such activities could be defensible?

Must not evaluation inherently empower authorities who, armed with their "regime of truth," wield it to coerce, oppress, and "terrorize" people? If sense can be made of the idea of a postmodernist "prescription," the prescription probably should be to jettison evaluation altogether.

Sensitive to this negative potential, Stronach and MacLure (1997) call for a "positive postmodern reading." (This is similar in motive if not substance to the move by Aronowitz & Giroux, 1990, who advocate a "critical" as opposed to "apolitical" postmodernism vis-à-vis education.) Although they are guarded in what they say, Stronach and MacLure commit themselves to the idea that postmodernism can have "practical" consequences for evaluation, which turns out to be the idea that incorporating postmodernist insights can make evaluation better. This is how they see the prevailing modernist view propounded by evaluators such as MacDonald (1977), Stake (1984), and House (1980):

> [These evaluation theorists] embodied modernistic . . . assumptions about the nature of knowledge and its relation to politics, a belief in progress, the possibility of a meta-perspective and usually an essentialist view of the role of the researcher or evaluator—as ethnographer, democratic evaluator, or critical theorist—as well as the need for apprentices to these roles to have lengthy and accredited training. (Stronach & MacLure, 1997, p. 102)

Given that postmodernists see knowledge as contingent, as growing from specific social circumstances, what are these determining contingencies for evaluation, in their view? Stronach and MacLure argue that evaluators in postmodern capitalism find themselves increasingly under the control of government agencies that insist on short-term contracts and closely managed studies. The studies, even the findings, often are owned by governments, resulting in incestuous relationships between policy and evaluation, as well as insecurity in the jobs of dependent evaluators. These are not the modernist conditions of independent scholars working dispassionately for truth, the way evaluators portray the situation.

> In addition, the overlapping regime of government sponsored institutional competition . . . incorporates an underlying research culture of competitive individualism within the disciplinary markets of the research economy. We need a more skeptical politics of the evaluator/researcher role and his/her less than innocent quest for knowledge, influence, and status. (Stronach, 1997, p. 33, in his deconstruction of qualitative evaluation)

Faced with such contingencies, these postmodern evaluators cast their strategy in terms of a particular kind of survey instrument they have employed, the "report and respond" questionnaire, which seeks "transgressive validity" in an attempt to breach borders. Concepts like "validity" are highly suspect, as normally construed, and are to be replaced by concepts like "transgressive validity" (Stronach & MacLure, 1997, p. 100).

Respondents to the survey are invited to make written comments not only in a typical, "any comments" section, but to fixed-response items as well. For example, here is an item:

> The following sources of support were appreciated by teachers: exchanging materials with course members [ ]; establishing new contacts [ ]; good support from college tutors [ ], from SEN advisers [ ], and through group tutorials [ ]. [Comments, additions?] (Stronach & MacLure, 1997, p. 105)

Respondents could respond in the boxes to agree or disagree with these conclusions, and could also add whatever comments they liked immediately following a particular conclusion. The interim report consists of many such conclusions/items. In a sense, respondents participated in constructing the actual interim evaluation report.

According to Stronach and MacLure, this methodological departure serves to blur the boundaries between formal and informal data, conforming to and breaching cultural conventions, summative and formative evaluation aims, and cognitive and affective kinds of responses. The normal categories of the "regime of truth" are "breached" deliberately. Presumably, this serves transgressive validity.

One of the "virtues" exemplified is a "revised notion of *negotiation*, or of *dialogue* between researcher and researched" that makes "interactions less asymmetrical in terms of power relations, [and] encourage[s] a more active and discrepant engagement of the researched in the research process" (Stronach & MacLure, 1997, p. 111).

> R&R [report and respond] is characterized by its *hybrid* nature. It is a questionnaire and an interim report, which both gathers and disseminates information. It offers judgement but solicits correction, treats respondents as both audience and informants, and regards the research process as an ambivalent mixture of engagement (provocative, analytical, dialogic) and detachment (separate from the actions of the respondents, interpretative). (Stronach & MacLure, 1997, p. 109)

In this survey, fully 80% of the respondents chose to respond in the "informal register" by adding commentary, often expressing emotional reactions, stimulated by the provisional nature of the questionnaire. Hence, the instrument served to provoke and promote more authentic dialogue indicating signs of "struggle," in the view of the postmodern evaluators.

The key (transgressive) validity question might be, What signs are there of the interventions by the respondents in the evaluators' text? Presumably, the better the interventions, the better the "transgressive validity," that is, the challenge to the regime of truth of the administrative agency sponsoring the evaluation. Negotiation with respondents occurs in the (knowledge-producing) middle of the evaluation report, rather than through their responding to a finished report at the end or negotiating an agreement at the beginning of the evaluation.

> For an educational researcher or evaluator, how can that be a bad thing? Does not the impetus implicit in not-knowing, in not-ever-knowing, in knowing something of the not-ever of knowing not represent the greatest and most fruitful challenge that students of education could ever wish? To be positive, then, accentuate the double negative? That would be looking on the bright side of postmodernism. (Stronach, 1997, p. 34)

What can we say about this postmodern view of evaluation? Certainly, the aim of achieving more authentic dialogue is one we endorse, and these postmodernist evaluators are inventive (a term not often applied to methodological endeavors). However, this "positive reading"—one that aims to provide voice for research participants on something approaching equal terms with evaluators— doesn't go very far. As with radical constructivism, in the absence of some further discussion of what balance should be struck between the evaluators' voices and participants' voices, such procedures might allow the most powerful voices to dominate and the special knowledge and expertise associated with evaluators qua evaluators to be underused.

This "positive reading" of postmodernism seems to be a form of democratic theory that prides itself on being deliberately fuzzy, disjointed, and unstable, and essentially negative. The rationale is that the "Other" (critical theorists, liberals, and so on) clings to "foundationalism," "essentialism," and all the rest, and therefore *must* endorse evaluators' exercising their power over others in a way that is ultimately undemocratic.

Although this indictment has some truth to it, contemporary democratic theorists—various liberals, critical theorists, and feminists—have moved a goodly way in recent years, largely in response to a growing recognition (spurred by postmodernist insights) of the contingent and variable nature of self-identity and the undemocratic results this can have when ignored.

A CRITIQUE OF POSTMODERNISM

The criticism that routinely leaps to mind is that postmodernism is hopelessly relativistic and self-defeating, that it cannot justify any knowledge claims whatsoever, if consistently held. If all knowledge claims are thoroughly context-bound and are simply masks for dominant interests and power, are not postmodernists themselves also possessed of these features? Aren't they simply masking yet other interests themselves? How can they escape?

A more positive critique expounds on how knowledge can indeed result from contingent beginnings. Many critics of postmodernism are committed to dialogical methods and join postmodernists in rejecting the traditional philosophical quest for ultimate epistemological touchstones that transcend contingent human experience. But for such thinkers, "overcoming epistemology," to use Charles Taylor's (1995, chap 1) phrase, does not entail characterizing knowledge as merely a mask for self-interest and power. Theorists such as Taylor see their task as working out defensible conceptions of knowledge and rationality that have contingent human experience as their basis.

Among these are pragmatists, critical theorists, and (certain) feminists. Thomas Kuhn (1962) provides the best general description of such a view when he likens it to Darwinian evolution. In short, in his view there exists no acontextualized criterion of knowledge toward which science must move. Instead, scientific theories are supported to the extent that they handle the problematic better than their competitors. Bootstrapping characterizes scientific knowledge. Criteria for making judgments exist, but they cannot be mechanically applied, have no ultimate foundation, and are not settled once and for all.

Kuhn's emphasis is on scientific "paradigms." There is also the less familiar and less discussed (outside philosophy) issue of moral epistemology. Michael Walzer (1983) distinguishes two ways of doing moral philosophy:

> One way to begin the philosophical enterprise is to walk out of the cave, leave the city, climb the mountain, fashion for oneself . . . an objective and universal standpoint. . . . Another way of doing philosophy is to interpret to one's fellow citizens the world of meanings we share. Justice and equality can conceivably be worked out as philosophical artifacts, but a just or an egalitarian society cannot. If such a society isn't already there—hidden, as it were, in our concepts and categories—we will never know it correctly or realize it in fact. (p. xiv)

Charles Taylor (1995, chap. 3) draws a distinction parallel to Walzer's between what he terms "apodictic" and "ad hominem" models of practical reason. The apodictic model requires that there be (a) some independent criterion uncontaminated by any particular system of beliefs, values, and dispositions against which to check the claims of practical reason and (b) some fail-safe procedure by which to determine whether the criterion is met. But such a criterion sets an impossible standard. Because it cannot be met, practical reason— reasoning that applies in morals and politics, as well as in evaluation and applied research—collapses into subjectivism and nihilism where moral and political claims are characterized as always and everywhere based upon mere "prejudice" or "bias"—much like the postmodernist position.

However, this conclusion follows only if there is no alternative way to construe practical reason (such as evaluative reasoning), and Taylor believes there is: the ad hominem model. Taylor begins with an observation about practical reason, that people rarely advance outrageous moral claims, and when they do, their real views are hidden and more complex, almost always qualified with some form of "special pleading" that excuses or redefines what is being advocated, as well as what it implies.

Consider the charge that cuts in welfare programs accompanied by cuts in capital gains taxes show a callous disregard for the poor, and consider the special pleading exemplified in the "trickle-down" response—"No, you are wrong, we really want to *help* the poor. Freeing up more capital is the best way to do it." Even the practical reasoning of the Nazis, Taylor (1995) observes, exhibited this pattern:

> [Nazis] never attack the ban on murder of conspecifics frontally. They are always full of special pleading: for instance, that their targets are not of the same species, or that they have committed truly terrible crimes which call for retaliation, or that they present a mortal danger to others. (p. 35)

Taylor uses the "special pleading" phenomenon, and the underlying agreement it implies, as the basis for the following picture of practical reason:

> The task of [practical] reasoning, then, is not to disprove some radically opposed first premise (say killing people is no problem), but rather to show how the policy is unconscionable on premises which both sides accept, and cannot but accept. . . . its job is to show up special pleas.
>
> On this model . . . practical argument starts off on the basis that my opponent shares at least some of the fundamental dispositions toward good and right which guide me. The

error comes from confusion, unclarity, or unwillingness to face some of what he can't lucidly repudiate; and reasoning aims to show up this error. (p. 36)

In the case of trickle-down economics, the job of reason is to show how its associated policies can only further damage the prospects of the poor; in the case of the Nazis, it is to show that their theories of racial superiority and perception of the Jewish threat are preposterous. (This is reason's "job"; whether it will win the day in either of these cases is another question.)

This conception of practical reason dovetails with the broader interpretivist epistemology of social research, and not only because both are "antifoundationalist." Interpretivists hold, contra positivism, that just as social science is irremediably theory-laden, it is irremediably value-laden as well. It is thus shot through with practical reason. In this way, the ad hominem strategy generalizes to evaluation. By contrast, the postmodernist attack on reason nullifies *all* knowledge claims, including any advanced by postmodernists themselves. As Benjamin Barber (1992) puts it:

Reason can be a smoke screen for interest, but the argument that it is a smoke screen itself depends on reason—or we are caught up in an endless regression in which each argument exposing the dependency of someone else's argument on arbitrariness and self-interest is in turn shown to be self-interested and arbitrary. (p. 109)

Generally speaking, ad hominem challenges such as the one exemplified by Barber are frequently employed against postmodernists to show that they cannot *both* have a moral-political project *and* disavow a commitment to reason. This is a difficult challenge for those who claim allegiance to postmodernism but nonetheless seek to get beyond merely deconstructing and disrupting social life in order to direct it in progressive directions—such as evaluators.

Similar problems confront the conception of democracy we associate with postmodernism: *hyper-pluralism*. This conception shares
with hyper-egalitarianism the view that truth and objectivity are
constructions that ought not be privileged, and that these concepts
apply no better to factual than to value claims. What most sets
hyper-pluralism apart from hyper-egalitarianism, as well as from
other conceptions of democracy, is its emphasis on encouraging and
enabling the expression of different views. For instance, in the *The
Postmodern Condition* (1984), Lyotard advocates supplanting "ho-
mology" (seeking consensus) with "paralogy" (activating difference).

Magnifying difference serves to disrupt taken-for-granted "regimes of truth" that are socially constructed and that embody standards of truth that privilege certain interests and marginalize others
by their very nature. Evaluation and social research, or their "paradigms," are presumably instances of regimes of truth. Thus, given
hyper-pluralism, it is difficult to conceive of evaluation in any way
resembling its present forms. Indeed, the institution of evaluation
seems to be exemplary of the kinds of norms and practices of
contemporary society that hyper-pluralism seeks to disrupt.

Because hyper-pluralism replaces the goal of forging agreement
with the goal of magnifying differences, it might be viewed as nondemocratic; perhaps, as we suggested earlier, it is *post*democratic. The
question of how to position hyper-pluralism vis-à-vis democracy
creates a fundamental problem. If hyper-pluralism eschews democracy, its advocates face the difficult task of defending some other
political arrangement. If the view embraces democracy, its advocates
face the task of explaining how to incorporate democratic decision
making: joint deliberation constrained by shared procedural rules.

In conclusion, in spite of rejecting postmodernism, we share three
points of agreement with postmodernists. First, subjectivities count.
How people see the world and themselves is very important. Second,
social arrangements are irremediably interest-laden, power-laden,
and value-laden. They need to be examined ("deconstructed") in this
light. Third, the goal of practices like evaluation should be a more

just and democratic society (although some postmodernists might disagree with this last view).

Sketching contemporary democratic theory and its advantages over postmodernist approaches (as well as the received view and radical constructivism) is a task we take up in the next chapter. We conclude this chapter with an observation about theory versus practice. These two variants of dialogical theory—radical constructivist and postmodernist—are fundamentally flawed. Their radical relativist epistemologies entail an evaluation practice that suffers from the moral-political inaction associated with hyper-egalitarianism and hyper-pluralism, at least if advocates are consistent. One way to avoid paralysis is to articulate concepts and principles—truth, justice, and democracy, for instance—that constrain dialogue and serve to distinguish authori*tative* from authori*tarian* claims.

Viewed in terms of avoiding authoritarianism, our differences with radical constructivist and postmodernist approaches may not be irreconcilable. We are advised by them to tread lightly, to be tentative, and to be highly suspicious of those who claim to know what is best. We are also advised to pay close attention to local social conditions and to individual "subjectivities." We do not deny the legitimacy of these concerns.

However, we insist that some moral-political principles are unavoidably presupposed in the practice of evaluation and that a critical articulation of such principles is important in the design and appraisal of evaluations. We acknowledge that under existing social and political conditions, compromise—and being compromised—is an unavoidable hazard. On the other hand—and this is the crux—there is no escaping this predicament by invoking the idea that values cannot be decided rationally and are beyond the scope of evaluators.

PART III

Deliberative Democratic Evaluation

6

THE DELIBERATIVE
DEMOCRATIC VIEW

———•◆•———

uring the 1980s, the Program Evaluation and Methodology Division (PEMD) of the U.S. General Accounting Office was the most highly regarded evaluation unit in Washington. Its director, Eleanor Chelimsky (1998), has provided a valuable summary of what she learned over her years as head of that office. One of her conclusions is that specific political conditions have strong effects on how evaluations are done. She also makes a strong point about advocacy:

> The need in a political environment is not for still another voice to be raised in advocacy, but rather for information to be offered for public use that's sound, honest, and without bias toward any cause. Policy makers in the Congress expect evaluators to play precisely such a role and provide precisely

this kind of information. . . . Yet we've seen recently attempts
to rationalize *advocacy by evaluators,* and this idea has some
roots in theory. . . . Our experience in PEMD was that advocacy of any kind destroys the evaluator's credibility and has
no place in evaluation. (p. 40)

At the same time, she says, Congress rarely asks serious policy
questions about Defense Department programs. She found this to be
especially true of questions about chemical warfare. In 1981, when
Chelimsky initiated studies on chemical warfare programs, she found
that there were two literatures. One was classified, favorable to
chemical weapons, and presented by the Pentagon in a one-sided way
to Congress. The other was critical, dovish, public, and not even
considered by congressional policy makers.

On discovering this situation, her office conducted a synthesis of
all the literature, she says, "which had an electrifying effect on
members of Congress who were confronting certain facts for the
first time" (p. 43). This initial document led to more evaluations,
publicity, and eventually contributed to international chemical
weapons agreements—a successful evaluation by almost any standards.

This chemical warfare work was predicated on analyzing the
patterns of partisanship of the previous research, understanding
the political underpinnings of the program and the evaluation, and
trying "to integrate conflicting values" into the evaluation—which
Chelimsky recommends for all such studies. This is a very intelligent
approach, it seems to us.

Our question is, What framework guided her to conduct the study
in this fashion? Why did she ask serious questions about Pentagon
programs when Congress did not? No stakeholder group was inciting
her to do so. The Pentagon pushed its own information, and the
antichemical doves theirs. Chelimsky had to have some framework,
intuitive though it might have been, for guiding her as to what to do.

We don't know what framework she actually used, but we think
one framework that could produce similar results would be some-

thing like this: Include conflicting values and stakeholder groups in the study. Make certain all major views are sufficiently included and represented. Bring conflicting views together so there can be deliberation and dialogue about them among the relevant parties. Not only make sure there is sufficient room for dialogue to resolve conflicting claims, but also help policy makers and the media resolve these claims by sorting through the good and bad information. Bring the interests of the presumed beneficiaries to the table if they are neglected.

All of this analysis and interpretation requires many judgments and decisions on the part of the evaluators as to who is relevant, what is important, what is good information and what is bad, how to handle the deliberations among policy makers, how to handle the media, what the political implications are, and so on. The evaluators unavoidably become heavily implicated in the findings, even if they themselves don't formulate the conclusions of the study. Their intellectual fingerprints are all over the place.

There are several points to be made here. One is that *some* framework is necessary to guide the evaluation, even if it is implicit. Second, the framework is a combination of facts and values. How the various groups thought about (valued) chemical warfare was an important consideration in the evaluation. Facts and values were joined together, just as they were in Stake's case study of a Chicago elementary school, cited earlier. Furthermore, Chelimsky's evaluation of chemical warfare is guided by a particular conception of the role of evaluation in public policy.

Is this advocacy on the part of the evaluators? We would say no, even though the work is heavily value-laden and incorporates considerable evaluator judgment. It is not advocacy in the sense of taking the Pentagon or the doves' side of the issue at the beginning of the study and championing only one side or the other. After all, if the Congress is so heavily slanted toward the Pentagon, it would make political sense to keep on their good side, because they are the clients. Presumably, this is what client-oriented evaluators would have done. Or they might have constructed value summaries such as those endorsed by Shadish, Cook, and Leviton (1995), "If you are in favor of chemical weapons, X is the action to take, but if you are opposed, Y is the action to take," and turned these over to policy makers.

But the evaluators did something more defensible—they included all sides in the study and evaluated the quality of each side's evidence by reference to critical counterclaims. This was the proper thing to do, in our view. The conduct of this study is consistent with the kind of evaluation theory we want to endorse. We suggest three general criteria for evaluations to be properly balanced in terms of values, stakeholders, and politics, in what we call the deliberative democratic approach. First, the study should be inclusive so as to represent all relevant views, interests, values, and stakeholders. No important ones should be omitted. In the chemical warfare case, the views critical of chemical warfare programs were omitted originally and only the favorable Pentagon views were included, thus biasing the conclusions in previous studies.

Second, there should be sufficient dialogue with the relevant groups so that the views are properly and authentically represented. Getting authentic views is not always easy, but it is often critical. "Paying attention to what the beneficiaries of a program think about it is a hallmark of a credible study, and has nothing to do with advocating for those beneficiaries" (Chelimsky, 1998, p. 47). Many studies have been conducted without the interests of the major beneficiaries (or victims) being included. In this case the potential victims of chemical warfare can hardly be present. Someone must represent their interests. Presumably, including stakeholders and talking to them when possible is *not* advocacy in Chelimsky's view.

Third, there should be sufficient deliberation to arrive at proper findings. In this case the deliberation was long and productive, involving evaluators, policy makers, and the media eventually. Deliberation might involve ways to protect evaluators or others from powerful stakeholder pressures, which can seriously inhibit discussion, as Chelimsky notes. Proper deliberation cannot be simply a free-for-all among stakeholders. If it is, the powerful stakeholders win.

Designing and managing all this involves considerable judgment on the part of evaluators. Evaluators can be guided by intuition, as Chelimsky and her colleagues seemed to be, or they can rely on something more explicit. Actually, Chelimsky advances a particular conception of the public interest, that is, that the evaluation should be judged by "its success as a provider of objective information in the public interest" (p. 52). And she goes further: "My guess is that the much greater risk to our field is not lack of use for the right reasons, but rather a declining capability or willingness to question conventional wisdom, which is our most important task and the best justification for our work" (p. 51).

So isn't she an advocate for her particular conception of the public interest and of evaluation's role in it? If not, how does this view differ from advocacy? Advocacy in one sense means taking the views or interests of one group and always championing them over others, regardless of the findings of the evaluation. For example, Chelimsky and her colleagues could have taken either the views of the Pentagon or those of the doves without balancing out the two. This would be one kind of advocacy. She hasn't done this.

On the other hand, if advocacy means using or endorsing *any* particular frameworks or values, Chelimsky might be accused of advocacy for her particular conception of the public interest, one not everyone would agree with. She says all evaluators should conduct evaluations with informing the public interest in mind. She might be an advocate in that sense of endorsing an overall framework. In fact, we believe that all evaluators must embrace *some* conception of the public interest and democracy, even if these conceptions are implicit.

In *this* sense evaluators should be advocates—for democracy and the public interest. Democracy aspires to incorporate all legitimate interests. In our view the public interest is not static and often is not initially identifiable, but emerges (or ought to) through properly constrained democratic processes in which evaluation plays a role. Interestingly, because evaluators *should be advocates* for democracy and the public interest, they *should not be advocates* for particular stakeholder groups in which perceived interests are viewed as impervious to evidence and are promoted come what may. (Greene, 1997, uses the term *advocacy* in one sense and Chelimsky, 1998, uses it in the other, so unfortunately they are talking at cross-purposes.) Nor should evaluators play the role of neutral facilitators among advocates of competing "value summaries" or stakeholder "constructions," in our view.

How does this chemical warfare case differ from evaluation of social programs? It differs very little. In Madison and Martinez's (1994) evaluation of health care services on the Texas Gulf Coast, they identified the major stakeholders as the recipients of the services (elderly African Americans) and the providers of the services (mostly white physicians and nurses), plus representatives from African American advocacy groups. Each group had a different view, with the elderly saying the services were not sufficiently accessible and the medical providers saying the elderly lacked knowledge about the services.

Is it advocacy to include particular groups, let's say the elderly African Americans in this case, in the study? We think it is not advocacy, but rather a balancing out of the values and interests in the study. All perspectives should be represented—the democratic view—and evaluators should try to determine who is correct. Nor is it advocacy to enter the study with the knowledge that African American views are often excluded in such studies. That is documented history, and evaluators should be alert to such possibilities.

In such an evaluation, there is no grand determination of the rights of elderly African Americans versus those of white professionals in society at large. That is beyond the scope of most evaluations. Evaluators must determine what is happening with these services in this place at this time, a more modest task. Advocacy in the misdirected sense would mean that the evaluators enter the study already convinced that the African Americans are right and the service providers wrong, or vice versa, regardless of the facts. This is not the proper posture for professional evaluators.

Our notion of the public interest in evaluation is one in which the evaluation informs public opinion objectively by including views and interests, promoting dialogue, and fostering deliberation directed toward reaching valid conclusions. Objectivity is supplied by inclusion, dialogue, and deliberation and by the evaluation expertise the professional evaluator brings to bear. Evaluators cannot escape being committed to some notion of democracy. The question is how explicit and defensible that notion is.

In the remainder of this chapter we explicate the deliberative democratic view, contrast it with other views, and sketch its connection to political theory. This view is not an evaluation model in the sense of how to do evaluation so much as it is a framework for ascertaining whether an evaluation is unbiased and objective with regard to value claims. Just as evaluations can be biased by poor data collection and errors of omission or commission, so too can they be biased in the sense of incorporating the wrong values, stakeholders, and interests. This framework militates against such biases.

DELIBERATIVE DEMOCRATIC EVALUATION

Deliberative democracy may be identified with *genuine* democracy— that is, with what democracy requires when properly analyzed and understood. In a sense, the term *deliberative democracy* is redundant, because democracy in the fuller sense requires deliberation, in our view. But the redundancy is worth preserving to avoid confusion about our emphasis. We use the modifier to focus attention on the decision-making procedures democracy requires and to avoid confusion with other conceptions of democracy.

Our intent is to present an overall framework for judging evaluations on the basis of their potential for democratic deliberation. There are three requirements for deliberative democratic evaluation: The evaluation must be inclusive, dialogical, and deliberative. We discuss each of these requirements in turn, although they are not easy to separate from each other entirely.

The Inclusion Requirement

The first requirement of deliberative democratic evaluation is the inclusion of all relevant interests. It would not be right for evaluators to provide evaluations only to the most powerful or to sell them to the highest bidders for their own uses, thus biasing evaluations toward particular interests. Nor would it be right to let purchasers revise findings, deleting parts of the evaluation they don't like or enhancing the findings with their own self-serving notions. These are conditions of use that evaluators should not condone.

Evaluation studies aspire to be accurate representations of reality, not fictional devices for furthering the interests of some over others, as in advertising or public relations, with the prize going to those who pay for the service. The interests of all stakeholder groups are central, and the interests of all relevant parties should be represented, as genuine democracy would require. If all the relevant interests are not included, the result is only a sham democracy in which some have been excluded.

Some of the biggest threats to evaluation are power imbalances. Such imbalances are endemic in society, and it is easy to see how they can disrupt and distort an evaluation. The powerful may dominate the discussion, or those without power may not be represented. There must be some rough balance and equality of power for proper deliberation to occur.

Evaluators must design evaluations so that relevant interests are represented and so that there is some balance of power among them, which often means representing the interests of those who might be excluded in the discussion, because their interests are likely to be overlooked in their absence. And, of course, deliberation should be based on discussion of merits, not on the status of participants.

Determining and weighing interests is extremely complex and uncertain, and often controversial. First, not all interests have the same moral force. Bhaskar (1986) distinguishes interests that attach to needs, the morally weightier type, from the larger array of interests as follows:

An interest is anything conducive to the achievement of agents' wants, needs, and/or purposes; and a need is anything (contingently or absolutely) necessary to the survival or well-being of an agent, whether the agent currently possesses it or not. Satisfaction of a need, in contrast to fulfillment of a want or purpose, cannot ever per se make an individual or group worse off. (p. 70)

Scriven (1991) advances a similar distinction in the context of evaluation specifically. He distinguishes "value assessment," in which needs, wants, and market preferences are treated indifferently, from "needs assessment," properly understood. "Needs," he says, "provide the first priority for response . . . just because they are in some sense *necessary,* whereas wants are (merely) *desired"* (p. 241). Needs are associated with a "level of urgency or importance" not possessed by wants, market preferences, and the like, according to Scriven.

We do not mean to suggest that distinguishing interests associated with needs from interests associated with wants is easy to do in the conduct of evaluations, or even always necessary. Still, the distinction is one to which evaluators should attend. However fuzzy or controversial in some cases, it is nonetheless quite real. In many cases it is easy to draw the line—for example, the interests in food, shelter, and health care versus the interests in early retirement or luxury automobiles.

The Dialogical Requirement

The second requirement of deliberative democratic evaluation is that it be dialogical. What complicates determining and weighing interests is that individuals and groups are not always able to determine their own interests when left to their own devices. They can be fooled or misled by the media, by powerful interest groups suppressing or "spinning" evidence, or by not having or exercising opportunities to obtain information. *Real* interests of an individual or group are not necessarily the same as *perceived* interests. Real interests might be defined this way: Policy X is in A's interests if A were to experience the results of policy X and policy Y and would choose the result of policy X rather than that of policy Y. Identifying "real" interests is critical.

Discovering real interests is a major task of dialogical interaction. Evaluators cannot assume automatically what the interests of the parties are. Perhaps the evaluators are mistaken. It is better to engage participants actively through dialogue of various kinds. It may be that through dialogue and deliberation stakeholders will change their minds as to what their interests are. After they examine findings and engage in argument and discussion with others, they may see their interests as different from those with which they began.

The embeddedness of evaluation in the social fabric makes dialogue critical. Participants and evaluators must identify the real issues and even create them in many cases. Evaluation findings are emergent from these processes. They are not waiting to be discovered, necessarily, but are forged in the evaluation and discussions of findings. As with the earlier example concerning whether or not the United States should switch to a parliamentary system, we must mull over the relevant arguments. This does not mean the evaluation finding is "unreal" because it is emergent and constructed, any more than a car is unreal because it is constructed.

To secure dialogue, evaluators must represent all interests fairly, engage in dialogical processes with participants, and deliberate extensively on the issues. In a sense we can imagine moving along the value-fact continuum from statements of preferences and values collected through initial dialogue, through deliberations based on democratic principles, to evaluative statements of fact.

There is a danger here that evaluators may be unduly influenced through extensive dialogue with various stakeholder groups, a threat Scriven (1973) noted long ago in his call for "goal-free" evaluation. Although we believe this threat to impartiality to be real, the greater danger is of evaluators' not fully understanding the positions, views, and interests of various stakeholder groups and misrepresenting these groups in the evaluation. So we are willing to trade the threat to impartiality for the possibility of evaluators' fully understanding stakeholder positions by engaging in extensive dialogue with stakeholders. And the threat to impartiality is blunted by inclusion and deliberation.

In some situations it may be that there is little danger of evaluators' misunderstanding stakeholder views. Perhaps in some product evaluations evaluators can posit the interests of typical consumers with a minimum of dialogue because the contexts of the studies may be precisely defined in advance. However, in most evaluations of complex programs and policies, understanding stakeholders and their positions is no easy matter. The interests of various groups may conflict, and the more complex the situation, the more dialogue is needed to sort it out. In this sense, product evaluations may be more a special case of evaluations than the paradigm case. And we conceive dialogue to be not only desirable but necessary in most cases.

The Deliberative Requirement

The third requirement of evaluations is that they be deliberative. Deliberation is fundamentally a cognitive process, grounded in reason, evidence, and principles of valid argument, an important subset of which are the methodological canons of evaluation. In many instances the authority of evaluators based on their special expertise plays a critical role in a deliberative democracy.

By contrast, the received view associated with "emotivist" or "preferential" democracy takes as given the preferences, values, tastes, and interests of citizens and finds ways to maximize those interests. Evaluators cannot question those preferences—they are simply given. Facts lend themselves to specialist determination, as in science, but values are chosen and cannot be dealt with rationally. Hence, the best evaluators can do is to satisfy preferences (maximize preference satisfaction), regardless of what the preferences are. Such reasoning leads to a conception of democracy in which preferences and values are unexamined.

Our view is one in which values are not taken as given but are subject to examination through rational processes. Evaluation is a procedure for determining values, which are emergent and transformed through deliberative processes into evaluation findings. Evaluation thus serves a deliberative democracy, one in which interests and values are rationally determined. And careful discussion and determination requires the expertise of evaluators.

To be sure, evaluation should not take the place of voting and other decision procedures in a democracy. Rather, evaluation is an institution that produces evaluation findings used in democratic decision processes. Evaluation informs voting and other authoritative decision procedures in democratic societies; it should not preempt them.

After all, evaluation is inextricably linked to the notion of choice: what choices are to be made, who makes choices, and on what basis. Evaluation of public programs, policies, and personnel is based on the notion of collective choice and on some sense of drawing conclusions on the basis of merit. By contrast, we can envision individuals weighing and balancing various factors and arriving at conclusions as individual acts. This is a model of consumer choice, essentially a market model, with many individuals making their own choices based on available information, and in which collective choice is merely the sum of individual choices.

But most public evaluations are not like this. The relevant interests and stakeholders have to be determined as part of the evaluation. And consumer choice is not the same as collective choice derived from collective deliberation. Collective deliberation requires a reciprocity of consciousness among participants and a rough equality of power if participants are to reach a state in which they deliberate effectively about their own collective ends.

A note on the evaluator's authority in these matters: It is useful to distinguish between power and authority. Evaluators should accept authority but not power. For example, A has power over B when A can affect B's behavior contrary to B's interests. But A has authority over B when B complies because A has influenced B through good reasons attached to B's own interests. Democratic deliberation exists when deliberations are discussions of merit that involve the interests of A and B or their collective interests. Hence, evaluators have authority in the sense that people are persuaded by the evaluation for good reasons.

The requirements of inclusion, dialogue, and deliberation overlap and crisscross in complex ways. For example, the quality of the deliberation is not separable from the quality of the dialogue, which, in turn, affects whether inclusion (as opposed to mere tokenism) is achieved. In general, the three requirements of inclusion, dialogue, and deliberation cannot be cleanly distinguished and applied independently. They affect and reinforce each other.

Still, distinguishing them from each other provides guidance. If the inclusion and dialogue requirements are met but the deliberative is not, all relevant interests might be represented (provisionally) but may be inadequately considered, resulting in erroneous conclusions (a problem for "constructivist" and "postmodernist" approaches). If the inclusion and deliberative requirements are met but dialogue is missing, interests and positions might be misrepresented, resulting in inauthentic evaluations based on false interests and dominated by those with the most power (a problem for the "received view"). Finally, if the dialogue and deliberative requirements are met, but not all stakeholders are included, the evaluation may be charged with being biased toward particular interests.

Deliberative democratic evaluation is an ideal worth pursuing, not something that can be achieved once and for all in any one study or fully captured. But then again, collecting, analyzing, and interpreting data in a bias-free manner so as to arrive at accurate findings is never perfect either. That is no reason for evaluators to stop trying to do the best they can. There are better and worse ways to conduct studies from the point of view of deliberative democracy.

A Typology of Views

Table 6.1 provides a summary of the various views we have discussed, considering how they conceive facts and values, what

TABLE 6.1 Views on Values

Positivist	Strict fact-value dichotomy. Facts can be based on pristine observations (foundationalism). Values are "metaphysical" and not subject to rational analysis. *Evaluator role:* determine facts, treat values as emotional expressions or individual preferences. *View of democracy:* emotivist or preferential with utilitarian calculus (i.e., values are determined by nonrational means or else all preferences are admitted to be maximized).
Early post-positivist (e.g., Campbell)	Explicit fact-value dichotomy; however, facts and theory cannot be determined by pristine observation because facts are theory-laden (nonfoundationalism). Facts can be determined by reference to the entire body of knowledge. Values must be chosen. *Evaluator role:* determine facts, accept program or policy values. *View of democracy:* emotivist or preferential.
Value minimalist (e.g., Shadish, Cook, & Leviton)	Implicit fact-value dichotomy, although some prescriptive values admitted. Facts can be determined nonfoundationally but value claims must be tied to values of stakeholders in value summaries, "X is good if you value Y." *Evaluator role:* construct value summaries, accept stakeholder values. *View of democracy:* emotivist or preferential.

TABLE 6.1 Continued

Radical constructivist (e.g., Guba & Lincoln)	Relativist about both facts and values. Facts and values are both constructions of individuals, because there is no objective reality. "Reality" must be negotiated among stakeholders. *Evaluator role:* Mediate constructions of reality among participants. *View of democracy:* hyper-egalitarian (i.e., all views count the same in reaching consensus).
Postmodernist (e.g., Stronach & MacLure)	Relativist about both facts and values. However, insider views are problematic because insiders themselves may be deceived by "regimes of truth." Society must be liberated by disruptive acts. *Evaluator role:* deconstruct conventional notions and disrupt power relationships. *View of democracy:* hyper-pluralist (consensus not desirable, proliferate diversity indefinitely).
Deliberative democratic (e.g., House & Howe)	No strict fact-value dichotomy. Facts and value statements lie on a continuum where they meld together in evaluation statements. Nonfoundationalist. Both facts and values can be determined by rational processes. Evaluative conclusions can be objective (unbiased). *Evaluator role:* determine fact-value claims objectively and impartially. *View of democracy:* deliberative (reach consensus through inclusion, dialogue, deliberation).

conceptions of democracy they hold, and how they envision the role
of the evaluator.

LOCATING DELIBERATIVE DEMOCRACY
WITHIN POLITICAL THEORY

Finally, how do these ideas about deliberative democratic evaluation
connect to contemporary political theory? To answer this question we
take John Rawls's (1971) "liberal-egalitarian" theory as our theoretical point of departure. Briefly, in this section we (a) describe liberal-
egalitarianism and compare it with its major competitors in the
liberal tradition; (b) entertain the criticism (advanced by postmodernists) that, because this view is insensitive to diverse group identities, it is ultimately oppressive and undemocratic; and, finally,
(c) sketch the revisions that contemporary liberal theorists (especially
Kymlicka, 1990, 1991) have offered to meet these criticisms.

Liberal-egalitarianism may be distinguished from its two major
competitors within the liberal tradition, libertarianism and utilitarianism, largely in terms of its conception of distributive justice.
Libertarianism maintains a strong presumption against any form
of involuntary distribution of social goods (goods such as health,
education, and income). Utilitarianism, by contrast, rejects this
presumption and requires active manipulation of social arrangements
so as to ensure that distributions of goods serve to maximize benefits.

For its part, liberal-egalitarianism also requires the manipulation
of social arrangements, but, unlike utilitarianism, it places constraints on the shape that the distribution of benefits can take. In
particular, social arrangements must be designed so as to tend toward
equality in the distribution of benefits. The effects of circumstances
that are arbitrary from a moral point of view (for example, who one's
parents happen to be) must be mitigated to this end, and at the
expense of maximizing benefits, if necessary. Distributions resulting
from the operation of markets (the libertarian distributive principle)
must be held in check as well.

Liberal-egalitarianism has dominated the liberal tradition (and political theory) since the publication of John Rawls's celebrated *A Theory of Justice* (1971), a book that provided concepts for earlier evaluation works (House, 1980). Of course, this Rawlsian view has not gone unchallenged, and the challenges have become piercing of late. In various forms, criticism of the so-called distributivist paradigm (Young, 1990) has come to occupy a central place (a criticism that applies with equal force to utilitarianism).

The basic criticism is this: Liberal-egalitarianism identifies the disadvantaged in terms of the relatively low share of social goods they possess. It eliminates disadvantages by implementing compensatory social programs, educational and otherwise. All this is conceived typically as requiring little input from those most affected. In this sense it assumes that the social goods to be distributed, as well as the procedures by which distribution will occur, are uncontroversial. In fact, the goods may reflect the interests of those who have been and continue to be in charge. For example, consider a sexist curriculum with which girls, but not boys, have great difficulty. It is not a solution to provide girls with help in mastering this curriculum so as to remove their *disadvantage*.

The preceding account points to the difficulty that has prompted liberal-egalitarians to change their theory—away from equality as a principle of distribution and toward equality as a principle of democratic participation. In what might be called the "participatory paradigm," the requirements of distributive justice and those of democracy are intertwined. Justice requires giving all an effective voice in negotiating goods and defining their own needs, particularly members of groups that have been historically excluded. As Kymlicka (1991) observes: "It only makes sense to invite people to participate in politics (or for people to accept that invitation) if they are treated as equals. . . . And that is incompatible with defining people in terms of roles they did not shape or endorse" (p. 89).

The relationship between justice and democracy has implications for evaluation, the aim of which is to improve practice. The distributivist paradigm implies a top-down, expert-driven view. Investigators look for maldistribution of goods, define group needs, and formulate policies and practices. These decisions are made in the name of equality. The views of beneficiaries are ignored. This approach incorporates too limited a view of democracy.

The participatory paradigm fits with a view of evaluation in which equality is sought not solely in the distribution of predetermined goods, but in the status and voice of the participants. Goods, along with needs, policies, and practices, are investigated and negotiated in collaboration, with democratic deliberation functioning as an overarching ideal. Here methodologically sound evaluation can play a key role.

Thus, the participatory paradigm seems more consistent with dialogical views than with technocratic ones. It sides with the received view against postmodern and constructivist views' rejection of the authority of evaluation, even as it sides with those views in the necessity of dialogue.

We should note that we are using *participatory framework* in the most general sense, not necessarily endorsing any particular participatory evaluation approaches (see Cousins & Whitmore, 1998, for a review of participatory approaches). Our conception of participation is linked directly to an egalitarian theory of democracy. Simple participation by participants in an evaluation does not necessarily ensure a truly democratic process. There must also be inclusion and deliberation. Some participatory activities might actually impede the other two. Nonetheless, participation and dialogue are critical to the attainment of deliberative democratic evaluation.

Earlier evaluation works reflected the liberal-egalitarian view in which the distribution of primary goods was to be accomplished within certain limits (see, e.g., House, 1980). Although this view provided for deliberation and inclusion, it did not adequately provide for dialogue as a fundamental part of evaluation as we are now conceiving it in the deliberative democratic view. Hence, it was open to charges of paternalism in which authorities, such as evaluators, determined the good for others. The deliberative democratic view aspires to bring participants into dialogue in fundamental ways, so that they can authentically represent their own interests—they might also determine what their own real interests are in the process.

GOOD PRACTICE

——•◆•——

E valuators conduct their work in concrete social circumstances, and we recognize that the deliberative democratic
view is too idealized to be implemented straightforwardly
in the world as it exists. An uncompromising commitment to such
an ideal would be impractical. However, just because the ideal cannot
be fully attained, that does not mean it cannot serve as a guide.

Evaluators should not ignore imbalances of power or pretend that
dialogue about evaluation is open when it is not. To do so is to endorse
the existing social and power arrangements implicitly and to evade
professional responsibility. It may be that the existing power arrangements are acceptable, but evaluators should consider this issue explicitly. The solution is for evaluators to face the issues as best they
can and adopt a position of democratic deliberation as an ideal for
handling value claims. In this conception evaluators are not passive
bystanders, innocent facilitators, or philosopher kings who make

decisions for others, but rather conscientious professionals who adhere to a set of defensible, carefully considered principles for enhancing inclusion, dialogue, and deliberation.

What we offer here is not an evaluation model that prescribes how to conduct an evaluation. It is more a middle-range theory that suggests that studies should be unbiased (objective and impartial regarding facts and values). Bias itself can never be fully eliminated, but there are many specific ways of reducing it. Any number of approaches or models of evaluation or individual studies could fit our middle-range deliberative democratic requirements.

In fact, several evaluators have advocated practices that are consistent in important ways with the views we endorse here, though they might differ in other respects, such as Stake's (1984) responsive evaluation, MacDonald's (1977) democratic evaluation, Proppe's (1979) dialectical evaluation, Scriven's (1980) objective value judgments, and Greene's (1997) advocacy evaluation, as well as the work of Fischer (1980), Weiss (1983), Bryk (1983), Mark and Shotland (1987), Garraway (1995), Karlsson (1996), Fetterman, Kaftarian, and Wandersman (1996), Alkin (1997), Schwandt (1997), and Cousins and Whitmore (1998), to mention some who have explored similar ideas.

For example, Mark and Shotland (1987) say, "In particular, in stakeholder approaches the evaluator's tasks include deciding whose questions to address. In contrast, in non-stakeholder approaches . . . it is simply assumed that the evaluator will address those questions the sponsor desires to have addressed" (p. 133). Alkin (1997) has emphasized stakeholder participation and selection as critical, and Cousins and Whitmore (1998) have suggested that the critical dimensions for participatory evaluation are stakeholder selection, depth of participation, and control of the evaluation process.

Even among those positions we have critiqued (e.g., Guba & Lincoln, 1989; Shadish, Cook, & Leviton, 1995; Stronach & MacLure, 1997), there are practices we endorse even when we don't agree with the theoretical justifications for them. Good practice is eclectic and informed by theory, not totally derived from it.

CRITICAL QUESTIONS

We operationalize our deliberative democratic view as 10 questions. The questions we would ask of evaluations are the following:

☐ Whose interests are represented?

☐ Are major stakeholders represented?

☐ Are any major stakeholders excluded?

☐ Are there serious power imbalances?

☐ Are there procedures to control power imbalances?

☐ How do people participate in the evaluation?

☐ How authentic is their participation?

☐ How involved is their interaction?

☐ Is there reflective deliberation?

☐ How considered and extensive is the deliberation?

Karlsson (1996) has conducted an evaluation that illustrates many of our concerns about dialogue, even if his study was more extensive than most. He evaluated a 5-year program that provided care and leisure services for children ages 9-12 in Eskilstuna, Sweden. The program aimed for more efficient organization of such services and the introduction of new pedagogical content, to be implemented through new School Age Care Centers. Politicians wanted to know how services could be organized and with what pedagogical content, what the centers would cost, and what children and parents wanted the centers to be—in essence, a formative evaluation.

A first step was to identify stakeholder groups and choose representatives from them, including politicians, managers, professionals, parents, and children. Karlsson then surveyed parents and interviewed other stakeholder groups on these issues:

❑ *Politicians:* What is the aim of the program?

❑ *Parents:* What do parents want the program to be?

❑ *Management:* What is required to manage such a program?

❑ *Staff unions:* What do the staff unions require?

❑ *Cooperating professionals:* What expectations are there from others who work in this field?

❑ *Children:* What expectations do the children have?

Data were summarized and communicated to the stakeholder groups in the condensed form of four different metaphors of ideal types of school-age care centers. The metaphors for the centers were "the workshop," "the classroom," "the coffee bar," and "the living room."

In the second stage of the evaluation the focus was on the implementation of the centers, 25 altogether, serving 500 students. In contrast to the "top-down" approach of the first stage, this part of the evaluation employed a "bottom-up" approach by first asking children how they experienced the centers. Next, parents and cooperating professionals were interviewed, then managers and politicians. Dialogue was achieved through the presentation to later groups of what the prior groups had said.

In the first two stages of the evaluation, the dialogue admitted distance and space among participants. In the third stage, the goals were face-to-face dialogue and the establishment of more mutual and reciprocal relationships. The aim was to develop genuine and critical dialogue that could stimulate new thoughts among different stakeholder groups and bring conflicts into open discussion.

Four meetings were arranged with representatives from stakeholder groups. To ensure that everyone could have a say, four professional actors played short scenes illustrating the critical questions and conflicts to be discussed. The actors involved the audiences in dialogues through scenarios showing the essence of problems (identified from the collected data) and enlisted audiences to help the actors solve or develop new ways to see the problems. About 250 representatives participated in four performances, which were documented using video cameras and edited to 20-minute video-tapes. These were used in later meetings with parents, politicians, and staff.

In Karlsson's view, the aim of such critical evaluation dialogues should be to develop deeper understanding of program limitations and possibilities, especially for disadvantaged groups. In this process the important thing is to enable the powerless and unjustly treated stakeholders to have influence. The evaluator has two responsibilities in making critical dialogue possible: to develop a theoretical perspective on the program and to cultivate critical inquiry. *Theoretical perspective* means not a complete model or explanation, but a framework that puts the evaluand in historical and political context for participants (Haug, 1996).

With such a perspective, the evaluation becomes a matter not only of putting together and presenting the opinions and the stand-points of the interest groups but of developing a better theoretical understanding of the context and the problems of the program. In this, the evaluator brings a critical perspective to bear. In Karlsson's view, the difficulty with dialogue as a strategy is that it demands that every interest group have enough resources for participation. There is a risk of achieving participation only by those who are resource-powerful.

OTHER EXAMPLES

Other evaluators have also invented ways of dealing with these issues. In this section we discuss our basic questions one at a time and point to particular evaluations that exemplify various of our criteria.

Whose Interests Are Represented?

Ordinarily, the evaluation is shaped between the evaluator and the client, the sponsor of the evaluation. The evaluator must take cognizance of whose interests are being represented. It goes without saying that poor people and those without power rarely sponsor evaluations. The presumed beneficiaries of programs also rarely do so. For example, those who are ill do not typically sponsor evaluations of medical services (though philanthropic organizations might), nor do the homeless shape evaluations of welfare.

Typically, evaluations are sponsored by government agencies and shaped by medical or welfare or education professionals. These participants all affect the design of a study, and evaluators must be aware of whose interests are shaping any given evaluation. The concerns and interests of all groups are not necessarily the same.

For example, in Karlsson's evaluation, he identified the major stakeholders and their concerns through extensive dialogue. Politicians, the sponsors, were concerned most with the economic efficiency of the program, managers with how the program could be directed, professionals with how the goals could be realized, parents with the care and security their children received, and the youths themselves with maintaining contact with their peers. All these concerns were legitimate issues for shaping the evaluation, and the evaluator needed to consider them in the design. Clearly, not all concerns can be met fully in any one evaluation. Choices must be made.

Are Major Stakeholders Represented?

It is a requirement of deliberative democratic evaluation that all major stakeholders should be included somehow. Democracies gain legitimacy by including the interests of all. Of course, evaluation studies cannot include the interests of every single individual stakeholder who might be affected. Such inclusion is impractical; studies always have financial and time limitations. One compromise is to include the interests of only major stakeholders in the program—that is, those whose interests are most at issue. Such selection requires judgment by evaluators as to who these might be, just as professional judgments are required in other aspects of the study.

Often evaluators can use representation rather than the direct involvement of every single stakeholder. For example, Alkin, Adams, Cuthbert, and West (1984) evaluated agricultural extension in eight Caribbean countries. The key stakeholders were the sponsor (the U.S. Agency for International Development), the University of West Indies Project staff, agricultural extension officials in participating countries, farmers and their representatives, and American academics involved in the project. The evaluation team represented these stakeholders by including an American agricultural economist, a West Indies academic, an Ohio State academic, and a UCLA evaluation expert. The West Indies participant assured one important stakeholder group of the trustworthiness of the evaluation, and the economist assured USAID that important technical issues would be addressed. Including stakeholders in the evaluation team is one way of addressing the issue of stakeholder representation, but it is by no means the only way.

Are Any Major Stakeholders Excluded?

Another important question concerns whether major stakeholder groups are not included that should have been. There have been many studies conducted in which not even the interests of the presumed beneficiaries of the program have been included (Chelimsky, 1998). Such an omission biases a study, or else there must be good reasons these interests are not included. (Perhaps the program is in its early trials and is too rudimentary for evaluators to see how it affects beneficiaries.)

If major stakeholders are not included, it is incumbent on evaluators to rectify the situation. For example, Hahn, Greene, and Waterman (1994) evaluated 11 public policy education projects funded by the

Kellogg Foundation. They held semiannual working conferences for project personnel in which discussions about the projects were encouraged (Greene, 1997). The evaluators deliberately represented the interests of citizens who were to be informed by these activities and who were not present at the meetings, thus raising questions with the program staff about the direction of their efforts as the program affected the public. Sometimes evaluators must represent the views of missing stakeholders, if necessary, even though it is better to have these groups represent their own interests where possible.

Are There Serious Power Imbalances?

Evaluators must recognize when there may be strong power imbalances that can bias the design and findings of the study, just as they must recognize when other forms of bias affect the findings improperly. Improper selection of criteria, improper weighting of criteria, and slanting conclusions and recommendations in certain directions are ways in which these power imbalances are likely to be manifested.

Of course, there are power imbalances in every human activity, and it is not the evaluator's duty to correct all these. Rather, it is the evaluator's duty to make sure strong power imbalances do not distort the study's findings—not an easy task. The evaluator must identify where imbalances threaten the integrity of the study. For example, in Karlsson's (1996) study, to facilitate dialogue and deliberation, he arranged a critical dialogue among all stakeholder groups in face-to-face meetings in which participants considered the findings. Here he had to be concerned about how power imbalances would affect the dialogue and deliberation. In this case we might expect that the politicians would dominate the discussions and that the youths would be least able to represent their interests. Major stakeholders may be represented in a study and still proper deliberation may not be achieved. Karlsson's solution was to hire actors who actively engaged the less powerful and more reticent stakeholders, even the children.

Are There Procedures to Control Power Imbalances?

Imagine a class in which one student does all the talking. Ideally, teachers want all students to have a chance to participate. It is incumbent on teachers to find ways to control such imbalances, and all good teachers know how to do this through various mechanisms. Likewise, evaluators need to redress power imbalances. This is particularly true in qualitative studies in which some individuals or groups provide most of the information. The information itself can be seriously out of kilter if particular people dominate. Evaluators need to have ways of controlling power imbalances to achieve proper deliberation.

In their review of participatory evaluation, Cousins and Whitmore (1998) note: "In our experience it has been those participants or stakeholders with power who have tended to resist evaluation findings which might be viewed as critical and significant. They hold the power to quash the report or to reshape it in ways that meet their own needs" (p. 20). Cousins and Whitmore raise ethical questions as to who owns the findings, who dictates use, how much misuse the evaluator can stand, and how the evaluator draws the line.

How Do People Participate in the Evaluation?

The mode of participation is critical. Stake (1986) explores the difficulties of communicating with stakeholders in his analysis of the Cities-in-Schools evaluation. The evaluators of this program simply could not conceive how to deal with the many stakeholders, and the evaluation suffered accordingly. How participation is organized is nearly as important as who is selected to participate.

For evaluation studies concerning primary goods such as food and shelter, perhaps extensive dialogue with beneficiaries is not as necessary as in other cases. Most groups want their share of primary goods. However, even in the case of primary goods, it may make quite a difference to participants how services are delivered and what they consist of. Dialogue may be important for understanding the issues. And for the evaluation of complex social services, such as education and welfare, dialogue is usually necessary because programs and policies can be defined in many different ways and can affect groups differentially.

There can also be improper participation. In evaluating a pilot program to reduce the dropout rate in Ontario, Cousins met with the program steering committee, mostly school administrators, to design the study (and recommended they add teachers to the steering group; Cousins & Earl, 1995). Stakeholders were given interview training; they then conducted interviews and coded the data. The evaluator drafted the report, which was revised by teachers before it went to the steering committee. From this experience Cousins concludes that it is better *not* to involve participants in highly quantitative data analysis (Alkin, 1997). It may be that participants simply can't handle some kinds of deliberation and analysis, and it is improper to expect them to. Democratic deliberation allows for the possibility that in a complex, specialized society, expertise may be critical. Specialists may have to perform certain tasks in order for proper deliberation to take place.

How Authentic Is Their Participation?

Whether participation is through mailed surveys, focus groups, or personal interviews makes a huge difference as to its authenticity. Who is present, who sees the results, and who asks questions are critical issues. Barry MacDonald used to ask government officials, "What causes you to lie awake at night and worry?" (see MacDonald & Sanger, 1982). Having just provided the information that their occupational role required, which typically meant protecting their organization, government officials were able to step out of role and give quite different assessments of their situations as individuals speaking personally.

In an ethnographic study, Dougherty (1993) conducted an evaluation of a welfare-to-work training program in which she established close, long-term contacts with welfare participants on an intensive personal level, thus making possible authentic interpretation as to how beneficiaries of the program reacted to their training. Participants had far more complex reactions to the program than authorities had anticipated, and they faced different sets of problems from those the program addressed. Of course, such intensive work is not called for in every study, but evaluators must be concerned about the authenticity of the data they are considering.

How Involved Is Their Interaction?

Typically, evaluators would want stakeholders to be extensively involved in a study at different stages, depending on what kind of study it is. This would allow them plenty of opportunity to engage in critical dialogues, to express views fully and reveal important information. In the first evaluation one of us conducted, questionnaires were mailed to all Chicago high schools inquiring about the extent of their services for gifted students. The survey forms came back from the Chicago schools' central office all completed exactly the same way and all bound up together. The evaluator decided it was necessary to involve participants in a different manner.

Participation can be very extensive. Pursley (1996) evaluated a network of four family support centers in New York in which program participants and paraprofessional staff were included as partners in the evaluation. They helped develop the evaluation questions and instruments and helped collect and analyze the data. In particular, the evaluation sought to include the contributions of lower-level staff (Greene, 1997). Involving stakeholders in the more technical aspects of an evaluation risks a compromise between representation of views and proper management of the technical procedures, as noted above. There are trade-offs. All interests should be properly represented in the evaluation, and the proper methodology should be employed to produce unbiased findings.

Is There Reflective Deliberation?

It is easy enough to see that evaluators must consider all aspects of the data, various types of data, and how the analyses play out. Evaluation findings should be well considered and deliberated on. Unfortunately, sufficient deliberation about findings is often lacking in the hurried final phase of producing an overdue report. Perhaps lack of fit between the data and the findings is the most common error in studies generally. The problem is compounded when many stakeholder groups are involved in an active manner. There is seldom enough time. More satisfactory forms of participation have yet to be invented.

For example, Morris and Stronach (1993) constructed a set of findings in summary narrative form and sent it to the participants in their study (cited earlier as a postmodern evaluation). After each statement of the findings, an open box enabled respondents to agree, disagree, or abstain from commenting on that particular finding. And participants were encouraged to make extensive comments as to how they interpreted events. In this way participants had some say in the findings, even though the findings were constructed by the evaluators (Stronach & MacLure, 1997). And the evaluators had some sense of the degree to which the stakeholders agreed with their conclusions; in effect, putting the two together established a confidence band around the findings.

How Considered and Extensive Is the Deliberation?

Of course, in general, the more extensive the deliberation, the better findings we would expect to emerge. On the other hand, which academic has not sat through hours of faculty meetings exhausted by the endless perambulations of colleagues to no productive end? No point is too small to be raised, no issue too tiny to ponder. For the most part, however, there is too little deliberation rather than too much.

Evaluators should try to build such deliberation into the designs of their studies rather than simply hope for it. Greene (1988) evaluated an employment program for youths ages 14 to 19. Initial discussions included the coordinator of the program, the head of the youth department, and the agency director. This step was followed by discussions with 15 stakeholders aimed at developing an evaluation design. The stakeholders included funders, other youth professionals, employers, board members, administrators, program staff, and the youths themselves. Considerable dialogue was conducted with stakeholders to shape the design.

Data were collected from questionnaires, interviews, and group meetings with stakeholders. A subgroup of stakeholders was involved in more intensive interactions about questionnaire development. When data were available, nontechnical narratives were shared with stakeholders. Stakeholders reacted to interim reports, and these insights were included in the final report (Alkin, 1997). This study incorporated an extensive deliberation process at all stages, most likely beyond what most studies could manage. How much deliberation is enough is a good question, but then so is the question about how sophisticated the data analysis should be.

In all these studies cited, there was concern about how and which stakeholder interests were included, what kind of dialogue was encouraged, and how deliberation leading to findings was achieved. The evaluations used different procedures to increase inclusion of stakeholder interests and the authenticity of stakeholder views and interests. No single procedure is clearly superior to others for achieving these goals. A whole range of new procedures to accomplish these tasks has yet to be invented and tested.

No doubt there are also trade-offs involved, and currently there are no clear rules for making them. Involving stakeholders at one stage may foster a power imbalance in the findings later on. Including stakeholders in the data analysis may decrease the technical quality of the study. Data collection, analysis, and findings can be biased, just as representation of stakeholder interests can be. There is considerable room for professional judgment as to how to design and manage these activities.

Nonetheless, these evaluations do attempt to include major stakeholder interests, ascertain authentic stakeholder views, and facilitate joint deliberation leading to valid findings. Let us admit that these procedures are more raw and untested than the technical data collection and analysis procedures developed over past decades. Much work needs to be done, and many evaluators will be less than comfortable blazing new trails. Perhaps gradual testing of new ideas by pioneers is the prudent path.

A HYPOTHETICAL EXAMPLE

Let's pursue a hypothetical example, one that is particularly contentious in American society: ability grouping in schools. Suppose that the Centennial School Board has just been taken over by an educationally conservative faction who see the pursuit of the current school administration and former school board as being too concerned with minorities in the school district. The new board would like to reinstitute ability grouping in the schools, which was eliminated under the old regime. Ability grouping is popular with the upwardly mobile professionals who work in the burgeoning local high-tech industry and with the academics who teach in the local university.

The new school board orders the superintendent to install ability grouping in the middle schools in language arts, math, and science, by a vote of six to three. The largest minority groups are recently arrived Hispanics from Central and South America and Hmong from Southeast Asia. Hispanic activists in the community are vocally opposed to the new policy, whereas the Hmong are silent. The mostly Anglo middle-class professionals and academics are vocally in favor.

The school superintendent, under fire himself from the new school board, believes that an evaluation of the new policy is called for. He asks the local university to conduct the evaluation. The university evaluators take on the study, knowing that it is politically loaded. How should they proceed, understanding the context of the program and the evaluation?

In general, evaluators are responsible for investigating the pertinent body of social research against which programs may be understood and compared. Evaluators are also responsible for interpreting such research and judging its merits. In doing this, they are required to be *objective* or *unbiased*, not in the sense of refusing to offer judgments of their own, but in the sense of grounding such judgments in defensible methodological and moral principles.

Rarely will programs or policies be so innovative that no pertinent research exists, and this is certainly true of ability grouping. Although contested, much of the research is critical of ability grouping on the moral and political grounds that it denies equal educational opportunity to students placed in low-ability groups (e.g., Oakes, 1985; Wheelock, 1992). On the other hand, this research has its own methodological weaknesses.

This information might create a problem for the evaluation. If an evaluator steadfastly believes that ability grouping is wrong and an unmitigated evil, then his or her evaluating the Centennial program would be a waste of time. The same is true should an evaluator steadfastly support ability grouping in whatever circumstance. In both cases the conclusion would be a fait accompli. This is not to say that whether or not to practice ability grouping is radically undecidable, but rather that an evaluation in either of the above circumstances would be inappropriate. Cases in which there is no disagreement about the defensibility of the practice do not need evaluation ordinarily; for example, requiring African Americans to attend racially segregated schools is not appropriate for evaluation.

For a program or policy to be a proper subject of evaluation, its moral acceptability and effectiveness must be open to question. However, it is asking too much of evaluators to have no opinions about programs or policies going into an evaluation. After all, often evaluators are experts in the areas being investigated. In the case of the Centennial program, so long as evaluators are able to suspend judgment, they might have an initial tilt toward or against the practice of ability grouping and still perform a good evaluation. The key to avoiding bias is ensuring that competing claims and evidence are portrayed evenhandedly.

In the deliberative democratic view, competing claims and evidence must be assessed against the requirements of inclusive representation, dialogue, and deliberation, paying special attention to groups that lack power. In the Centennial evaluation, it would be important to alert stakeholders, especially the Hispanic and Hmong minorities, to research that indicates minorities are often disproportionately represented in low-ability groups and that being in a low-ability group is associated with low self-esteem as well as diminished opportunities for higher education and desirable employment.

Clearly, the interests of the new school board, those of the minorities, those of the opposition on the school board, those of the administrators, those of the teachers, those of the parents, and those of the children themselves should be included. Is there a more general public interest at issue? Does the society or the state have an interest at issue? It is not clear at this point.

There are several ways the evaluators can represent these stakeholders in the evaluation, from surveying them individually to involving them in the data collection, and still maintain proper balance. Surely, minority views are important in this case, and the minorities are unlikely to volunteer to work on the evaluation, especially the Hmong. If the evaluators open the evaluation to those who can work on data collection, the Anglo professional class will almost certainly dominate.

Certainly the interests of those in the professional class are important, but should these stakeholders be allowed to have a role in conducting the evaluation, too, thus increasing their already powerful influence? The evaluators must make some judgments about how much influence to allow each stakeholder group. It is not as if the evaluators can escape this issue.

On the other hand, the evaluators cannot presume to know the opinions of the minority members of this community without talking to the people themselves. Can they talk to the people and get an authentic representation of their views and interests? Members of these groups may be shy of public authorities for the most part. The evaluators might decide to involve the leaders of the minority groups, fully aware that they might not represent the real interests of their constituencies, any more than politicians represent the real interests of the public. Yet this is the compromise they might settle for under the circumstances. Evaluators must face practical limitations.

The evaluators arrange interviews with all members of the school board, the leaders of minority groups, the superintendent and his key staff, and the leaders of the parent groups. Clearly, the children's interests are most critical here, but can the children express informed opinions about ability grouping? In this age group, the evaluators think not. They think they have covered the major stakeholders. There is the business community, of course, but the evaluators cannot see how their interests are affected to the same degree on this particular issue.

Also, there is the public interest at large. Does ability grouping affect the public in a significant way? Does it increase inequality more generally in the society in a way that affects the public interest, or is it critically important that schools develop the future scientists necessary for the national welfare? If this evaluation involved the consideration of a policy for the entire nation, the evaluators might be more concerned about these issues. But they doubt that the national interest can be addressed simply in Centennial solely. Of course, these are tough professional decisions.

The evaluators must take some care to interview and record the interests of the various stakeholder groups and to ensure that the views represented are authentic. It would also be advisable for them to survey the parents of the students in some way, and not assume that the factions on the school board represent all the interests of the parents at large. Of course, this is difficult and expensive to do. Perhaps the evaluators might settle for meeting with local groups of parents in different parts of the school district. This risks misrepresentation, but a full-scale survey of the entire district would be too costly.

From all this information, the evaluators arrive at criteria for the evaluation: educational achievement, composition of the ability groups, social consequences, and educational opportunities gained or foreclosed in the future. It is advisable for the evaluators to check these criteria out with the various stakeholder groups to ascertain whether anything important is missing. The point is not to obtain agreement among the groups but to inform the evaluation itself. We presume that there is a right or wrong set of conclusions here, and that obtaining consensus is not the aim of the evaluation. The evaluators could obtain agreement and be wrong.

How should the various groups participate in the evaluation? There are many possibilities, as indicated by the earlier examples, but the evaluators might deliberately choose to do the data collection and analysis using a professional evaluation staff to avoid complaints further down the line that the results are contaminated somehow. They anticipate that the findings will emerge in a highly politicized situation and thus must be defensible from a methodological point of view. If the evaluators let some groups participate in certain aspects of the study, the entire study may be called into question.

After the findings are in, the evaluators will be involved in critical deliberations about them. If they simply present the findings to the school board, there is a good chance they will be accepted or rejected by a six to three vote, without sufficient consideration. Perhaps a better procedure would be for the evaluators to arrange neighborhood meetings in the local schools and present the findings to small groups of parents and civic groups prior to media presentation. These groups could then have time and guidance to consider at some length what they would gain and lose with ability grouping. Finally, the evaluators might conduct a formal presentation of the findings to the entire school board, with appropriate media coverage.

From that point it will be up to the school board, the school administration, the parents, and the media as to what decisions are made about ability grouping. The evaluators will have done their job of conducting an evaluation concerning the worth of ability grouping, and it is not their job to make decisions for the school district. They may have a further informational role, or they may not. In any case, they have scouted out the relevant issues, conducted the evaluation, and arrived at conclusions by including the appropriate views and interests, engaging in authentic dialogue, and arranging for sufficient deliberation on everyone's part.

Of course, all of this is imperfect from a theoretical point of view. The evaluators have not included every major group perhaps, or allowed sufficient time for deliberation, or secured the authentic views of some minorities perhaps. Such is the imperfect world of evaluation practice. No study has ever been done that cannot be criticized. What these evaluators can say is that they have made strenuous efforts to live up to deliberative democratic principles and that the resulting information has provided a much better basis for public understanding and decision than would be available in the absence of the evaluation.

CONCLUSION

The Role of Evaluation in Society

————•◆•————

We have presumed throughout our discussion in this volume that evaluation ought to serve democracy. Rather than defending democracy as such, we have assumed the more modest task of explicating and critically examining alternative conceptions of democracy that are incorporated into major approaches to evaluation, particularly conceptions exemplified by the received view, radical relativism, postmodernism, and the deliberative democratic view. In this conclusion, we revisit and amplify our major themes concerning evaluation in democracies.

We frame our discussion with three questions: What kind of democracy should we have? What characteristics of evaluation as a practice foster genuine democratic deliberation? And what are the characteristics of evaluators who engage in such deliberation?

DELIBERATIVE DEMOCRACY

Democratic, advanced capitalist societies have evolved formidable, sophisticated institutions of advertising, public relations, and mass media. The claims and counterclaims for products, programs, policies, and performance fly so thick and fast that citizens often cannot distinguish what is true from what is not. Even democratic politics is swept into media advertising campaigns in which 30-second sound bites supplant reasoned debate. Too often, serious politics becomes paid advertising.

To the degree that such societies depend on the reasoned judgments of their citizens (and we believe they do), social well-being is threatened by the chaos and confusion these new social dynamics of the mass media generate. The existence of institutions, such as evaluation, that provide sound knowledge about critical issues in society, including what products, programs, policies, and performance are worthwhile, becomes imperative. With sound knowledge as a basis, citizens can make informed judgments about public issues without being deceived, deluded, or confused.

Average citizens can no more collect data and conduct their own evaluations than they can design and construct their own flu vaccines. They need specialized assistance, and fortunately it is available in the form of institutionalized evaluation. To be sure, by recognizing the desirability and even the necessity of an institution that produces professional value conclusions, we risk being at the mercy of fraud and incompetence, but the benefits of professional evaluation are worth the risk, just as they are for professional medicine and law.

Two assumptions prevalent in emotivist (or preferential) conceptions of democracy are rejected in our deliberative (or cognitivist) view. One is that citizens in democracies are responsible only to the fulfillment of their own preferences, rather than to their notions of what should be done more generally (Hurley, 1989). In the emotivist view, the aim of democratic institutions is to elicit the preferences of citizens, then find ways to fulfill these preferences and regulate conflicts among them, where necessary. The second notion we reject is that democracy should be independent of any particular conceptions of the good life or what gives value to life. Hence, democratic institutions should not collect and summarize individual preferences only, regardless of what these are. The contents of the preferences make a critical difference. Some preferences may be undemocratic.

In the deliberative democratic view, citizens should express their beliefs about what should be done, not just fulfill their own preferences, and democratic institutions should provide the means of arriving at knowledge of what should be done. This knowledge should be true and objective in the sense we have employed here, even though truth is not always easily ascertainable. And knowing what is *not* true may be as valuable as knowing what is. It should also be clear by now that *objective* does not mean *value-neutral*.

Hence, in our view, it makes sense to have a division of epistemic labor to facilitate deliberation of public issues in a democracy. These cognitive institutions should promote deliberation and help citizens form accurate beliefs about what should be done. The result should be social self-determination, determination through collective deliberation, and not just individual self-determination.

Certainly, such an epistemic division of labor should not supplant other democratic forms of decision making, such as exercising decisions through voting or buying in markets. Rather, it should supplement other decision processes by educating citizens as to social worth. Rather than basing decisions on their a priori values, citizens may come to realize that their values have changed in the course of deliberation and that they now see their own self-interest in a different way, perhaps in a more public way.

In a sense, our idea of the societal role of evaluation is an extension of that advanced by Donald Campbell in earlier days. In a less contentious time, Campbell proposed that evaluators discover the efficacy of social programs that might improve society. The difference is that he thought we had simply to choose what values to support; there was no way of arriving at such values through reason.

In a more contentious time, we propose that evaluation help inform what those values (and evaluations) should be through reasoned processes framed by democratic concepts and principles, these concepts and principles themselves being subject to argument, debate, and revision. In our view there is no hard-and-fast separation of facts, which evaluation can determine, and values, which it cannot. Because facts and values are not two separate domains, evaluation can help determine conclusions that are blends of both.

CHARACTERISTICS OF EVALUATION

For evaluation to be a practice (or institution) that facilitates effective democratic deliberation about social programs, it must have a defensible (though not necessarily uncontroversial) conception of democracy. We have argued that emotive democracy, hyper-egalitarianism, and hyper-pluralism are not adequate. Each fails to redress power imbalances that seriously compromise democratic deliberation. By embracing the undecidability of values thesis in some form, each misconstrues the epistemological status of values and the role values play in evaluation studies.

We reject the undecidability of value thesis, and thus have no reason to refrain from offering arguments and making judgments regarding the merits of competing conceptions of democracy in developing the deliberative democracy view. This view interweaves an egalitarian (or needs-based) conception of justice that seeks to equalize power in arriving at evaluative conclusions. To recap, this view has three general requirements: inclusion, dialogue, and deliberation. These requirements are overlapping and interdependent, and each has a "thick" meaning tailored to fit the manifest inequality that characterizes contemporary society.

Inclusion requires that stakeholders be included in more than name only, as more than mere tokens whose voices are not heard or are heard but not taken seriously. The requirement of dialogue extends this conception of inclusiveness. Dialogue goes beyond having different views heard to include processes of give-and-take that enhance mutual understanding and refine the participants' own views. The requirement of deliberation focuses the dialogue on the objects of evaluation and constrains the dialogue in terms of evaluative reasoning, utilizing the methodological canons of evaluation to their fullest.

The deliberative democratic view is intended to apply to evaluation generally, as an *institution*, not only to given evaluation settings and participants. We believe that the disciplined and methodologically sophisticated perspectives that evaluation can apply to complex social problems can improve democratic deliberation dramatically. In an era of sound bites and of indiscriminate collapsing of various claims into the category of "special interests"—where the claims of bankers, tobacco growers, the poor, and women are all treated similarly—evaluation can play a crucial watchdog role.

But this role requires that evaluation embrace the moral-political direction provided by a deliberative democratic view. In advancing this view, we may be charged with infecting evaluation with partisanship and bias. However, the only way to sustain such a claim is to argue that values are not decidable to begin with, to presuppose that *any* view that incorporates substantive values *must* be partisan and biased. It does not follow from the fact that we offer a substantive value framework with which some disagree that we are wrong, much less that there is nothing to be right or wrong about. Any approach to evaluation is unavoidably committed to *some* conception of the relationship between evaluation and democracy. The key question to be asked is, How adequate is this conception?

CHARACTERISTICS OF EVALUATORS

Evaluators should be competent in social research methodology, including the special skills and knowledge required to perform credible evaluations; they should be familiar with the history and ethics of their craft and should have other characteristics typically included on such lists. In addition, there are several characteristics worth emphasizing vis-à-vis the deliberative democratic view.

First, evaluators have a fiduciary responsibility to participants in evaluations and to the public at large to use their office and expertise to further the public interest and communicate their findings in accessible ways. Because evaluators possess special knowledge and expertise, as well as special authority, they have a duty not to abuse their authority so as to deceive the public or surreptitiously promote their own agendas or the agendas of others. Like physicians, who are constrained by the value of promoting health, evaluators are constrained by the value of promoting democracy.

In this sense evaluators should be advocates for democracy and the public interest, and for what this presupposes, an egalitarian conception of justice. In our view the public interest is not static and often not initially identifiable, but emerges (or ought to) through properly constrained democratic processes in which evaluation plays a role. Because evaluators should be advocates for democracy and the public interest, they should not be advocates for particular stakeholder groups in which perceived interests are viewed as impervious to evidence and are promoted come what may. Nor should evaluators play the role of neutral facilitators without regard to democratic consequences.

Second, evaluators must be savvy negotiators, willing to engage in compromise. But, on pain of being mere functionaries doing the bidding of the powers that be, they must set limits as to how far compromise can go and be *un*compromising about unwarranted, self-serving, and morally objectionable claims that stakeholders might advance. Doing only what is practical is not sufficient.

Third, evaluators must take stands on moral-political fundamentals. And they must do so independent of stakeholders, if necessary. They should not permit clients and sponsors alone to determine whether and what values are considered in evaluations (House, 1993). All values should be subject to review.

We end this book with what will appear a bold statement to many: Evaluation is as good or bad as the value framework that constrains it, in the same way that it is as good or bad as the research methodology it employs. In fact, the two cannot be disentangled.

REFERENCES

———•◆•———

Alkin, M. C. (1997). Stakeholder concepts in program evaluation. In A. Reynolds & H. Walberg (Eds.), *Evaluation for educational productivity.* Greenwich, CT: JAI.

Alkin, M. C., Adams, K. A., Cuthbert, M., & West, J. G. (1984). *External evaluation report of the Caribbean Agricultural Extension Project: Phase II.* Minneapolis: Caribbean Agricultural Extension Project.

Aronowitz, S., & Giroux, H. A. (1990). *Postmodern education: Politics, culture, and social criticism.* Minneapolis: University of Minnesota Press.

Ayer, A. J. (1936). *Language, truth and logic.* New York: Dover.

Barber, B. (1992). *An aristocracy of everyone.* New York: Ballantine.

Bhaskar, R. (1986). *Scientific realism and human emancipation.* London: Verso.

Bryk, A. S. (Ed.). (1983). Stakeholder-based evaluation [Special issue]. *New Directions for Program Evaluation, 17.*

Campbell, D. (1974, September). *Quantitative knowing in action research.* Kurt Lewin Award Address, Society for the Psychological Study of Social Issues, presented at the meeting of the American Psychological Association, New Orleans.

Campbell, D. (1982). Experiments as arguments. In E. R. House, S. Mathison, J. A. Pearsol, & H. Preskill (Eds.), *Evaluation studies review annual* (Vol. 7, pp. 117-128). Beverly Hills, CA: Sage.

Chelimsky, E. (1998). The role of experience in formulating theories of evaluation practice. *American Journal of Evaluation, 19,* 35-55.

Constas, M. A. (1998). The changing nature of educational research and a critique of postmodernism. *Educational Researcher, 27*(2), 26-33.

Cousins, J. B., & Earl, L. M. (1995). *Participatory evaluation in education: Studies in evaluation use and organizational learning.* London: Falmer.

Cousins, J. B., & Whitmore, E. (1998). Framing participatory evaluation. In E. Whitmore (Ed.), Understanding and practicing participatory evaluation [Special issue]. *New Directions in Evaluation, 80,* 5-23.

139

Dougherty, K. C. (1993). *Looking for a way out: Women on welfare and their educational advancement.* Unpublished doctoral dissertation, University of Colorado, Boulder.

Fay, B. (1975). *Social theory and political practice.* London: Unwin Hyman.

Fetterman, D., Kaftarian, S. J., & Wandersman, A. (Eds.). (1996). *Empowerment evaluation: Knowledge and tools for self-assessment and accountability.* Thousand Oaks, CA: Sage.

Fischer, F. (1980). *Politics, values, and public methodology: The problem of methodology.* Boulder, CO: Westview.

Foucault, M. (1987). Questions of method: An interview with Michel Foucault. In K. Baynes, J. Bohman, & T. McCarthy (Eds.), *After philosophy: End or transformation?* (pp. 100-117). Cambridge: MIT Press.

Fournier, D. M. (1995). Establishing evaluative conclusions: A distinction between general and working logic. In D. M. Fournier (Ed.), Reasoning in evaluation: Inferential links and leaps [Special issue]. *New Directions for Evaluation, 68,* 15-32.

Frankena, W. J. (1967). Value and valuation. In P. Edwards (Ed.), *Encyclopedia of philosophy* (Vol. 8, pp. 229-232). New York: Macmillan.

Garraway, G. B. (1995). Participatory evaluation. *Studies in Educational Evaluation, 21,* 85-102.

Greene, J. C. (1988). Stakeholder participation and utilization in program evaluation. *Evaluation Review, 12,* 91-116.

Greene, J. C. (1997). Evaluation as advocacy. *Evaluation Practice, 18,* 25-35.

Guba, E. G., & Lincoln, Y. S. (1989). *Fourth generation evaluation.* Newbury Park, CA: Sage.

Gutmann, A. (1987). *Democratic education.* Princeton, NJ: Princeton University Press.

Hahn, A. J., Greene, J. C., & Waterman, C. (1994). *Educating about public issues.* Report from the Kellogg Foundation, Cornell University, Ithaca, NY.

Haug, P. (1996). Evaluation of government reforms. *Evaluation, 2,* 417-430.

House, E. R. (1980). *Evaluating with validity.* Beverly Hills, CA: Sage.

House, E. R. (1990). Realism in research. *Educational Researcher, 20*(5), 2-9.

House, E. R. (1993). *Professional evaluation: Social impact and political consequences.* Newbury Park, CA: Sage.

House, E. R. (1997). The problem of values in evaluation. *Evaluation Journal of Australasia, 8*(1), 3-14.

House, E. R., & Howe, K. R. (1998). Advocacy in evaluation. *American Journal of Evaluation, 19,* 233-236.

Howe, K. R. (1985). Two dogmas of educational research. *Educational Researcher, 14*(8), 10-18.

Howe, K. R. (1988). Against the quantitative-qualitative incompatibility thesis (or dogmas die hard). *Educational Researcher, 17*(8), 10-16.

Howe, K. R. (1992). Getting over the quantitative-qualitative debate. *American Journal of Education, 100,* 236-256.

Howe, K. R. (1995). Democracy, justice and action research: Some theoretical developments. *Educational Action Research, 3,* 347-349.

Howe, K. R. (1998). The interpretive turn and the new debate in education. *Educational Researcher, 27*(8), 13-20.

Hume, D. (1978). *A treatise of human nature.* Oxford: Oxford University Press. (Original work published 1739)

Hurley, S. L. (1989). *Natural reasons: Personality and polity.* New York: Oxford University Press.

Karlsson, O. (1996). A critical dialogue in evaluation: How can interaction between evaluation and politics be tackled? *Evaluation, 2,* 405-416.

Karlsson, O. (1998). Socratic dialogue in the Swedish political context. In T. A. Schwandt (Ed.), Scandinavian perspectives on the evaluator's role in informing social policy [Special issue]. *New Directions for Evaluation, 77,* 21-38.

Kuhn, T. S. (1962). *The structure of scientific revolutions.* Chicago: University of Chicago Press.

Kuhn, T. S. (1977). *The essential tension.* Chicago: University of Chicago Press.

Kymlicka, W. (1990). *Contemporary political theory: An introduction.* New York: Oxford University Press.

Kymlicka, W. (1991). *Liberalism, community and culture.* New York: Oxford University Press.

Lindblom, C. E. (1977). *Politics and markets.* New York: Basic Books.

Lyotard, J.-F. (1984). *The postmodern condition: A report on knowledge* (G. Bennington & B. Massumi, Trans.). Minneapolis: University of Minnesota Press.

Lyotard, J.-F. (1987). The postmodern condition. In K. Baynes, J. Bohman, & T. McCarthy (Eds.), *After philosophy: End or transformation?* (pp. 67-94). Cambridge: MIT Press.

Mabry, L. (1997). (Ed.). *Evaluation and the postmodern dilemma.* Greenwich, CT: JAI.

MacDonald, B. (1977). A political classification of evaluation studies. In D. Hamilton (Ed.), *Beyond the numbers game* (pp. 224-227). London: Macmillan.

MacDonald, B., & Sanger, J. (1982). Just for the record? Notes towards a theory of interviewing in evaluation. In E. R. House, S. Mathison, J. A. Pearsol, & H. Preskill (Eds.), *Evaluation studies review annual* (Vol. 7, pp. 175-198). Beverly Hills, CA: Sage.

MacIntyre, A. (1981). *After virtue.* Notre Dame, IN: University of Notre Dame Press.

Madison, A., & Martinez, V. (1994, November). *Client participation in health planning and evaluation: An empowerment education strategy.* Paper presented at the annual meeting of the American Evaluation Association, Boston.

Mark, M. M., & Shotland, L. R. (1987). Stakeholder-based evaluation and value judgments. In D. Cordray & M. W. Lipsey (Eds.), *Evaluation studies review annual* (Vol. 11, pp. 131-151). Newbury Park, CA: Sage.

Morris, B., & Stronach, I. (1993). *Evaluation of the management of change: Tayside TVEI.* Stirling, Scotland: University of Stirling, Department of Education.

Nozick, R. (1974). *Anarchy, state, and utopia.* New York: Basic Books.

Oakes, J. (1985). *Keeping track.* New Haven, CT: Yale University Press.

Phillips, D. C. (1983). After the wake: Postpositivistic educational thought. *Educational Researcher, 12*(5), 4-12.

Proppe, O. (1979). *Dialectical evaluation.* Urbana, IL: Center for Instructional Research and Curriculum Evaluation.

Pursley, L. C. (1996). *Empowerment and utilization through participatory evaluation.* Unpublished doctoral dissertation, Cornell University.

Quine, W. V. (1962). *From a logical point of view* (2nd ed.). Cambridge, MA: Harvard University Press.

Quine, W. V. (1970). The basis of conceptual schemes. In C. Landesman (Ed.), *The foundations of knowledge* (pp. 160-172). Englewood Cliffs, NJ: Prentice Hall.

Rabinow, P., & Sullivan, W. (1979). The interpretive turn: Emergence of an approach. In P. Rabinow & W. Sullivan (Eds.), *Interpretive social science* (pp. 1-21). Los Angeles: University of California Press.

Rawls, J. (1971). *A theory of justice.* Cambridge, MA: Belknap.

Rogers, P., & Owen, J. (1995, November). *Sources of criteria in evaluations.* Talk delivered at the University of Colorado, Boulder, School of Education.

Rorty, R. (1979). *Philosophy and the mirror of nature.* Princeton, NJ: Princeton University Press.

Rorty, R. (1982). Method, social science and social hope. In R. Rorty, *Consequences of pragmatism.* Minneapolis: University of Minnesota Press.

Schwandt, T. A. (1997). Evaluation as practical hermeneutics. *Evaluation, 3,* 69-83.

Scriven, M. (1969). Logical positivism and the behavioral sciences. In P. Achenstein & S. Barker (Eds.), *The legacy of logical positivism* (pp. 195-210). Baltimore: John Hopkins University Press.

Scriven, M. (1972). Objectivity and subjectivity in educational research. In L. G. Thomas (Ed.), *Philosophical redirection of educational research* (pp. 94-142). Chicago: National Society for the Study of Education.

Scriven, M. (1973). Goal-free evaluation. In E. R. House (Ed.), *School evaluation* (pp. 319-328). Berkeley, CA: McCutchan.

Scriven, M. (1980). *The logic of evaluation.* Inverness, CA: Edgepress.

Scriven, M. (1986). New frontiers of evaluation. *Evaluation Practice, 7,* 7-44.

Scriven, M. (1991). *Evaluation thesaurus.* Newbury Park, CA: Sage.

Scriven, M. (1994). The final synthesis. *Evaluation Practice, 15,* 367-382.

Shadish, W., Cook, T., & Leviton, L. (1995). *Foundations of program evaluation.* Thousand Oaks, CA: Sage.

Stake, R. E. (1984). Program evaluation, particularly responsive evaluation. In G. F. Madaus, M. Scriven, & D. L. Stufflebeam (Eds.), *Evaluation models* (pp. 287-310). Boston: Kluwer-Nijhoff.

Stake, R. E. (1986). *Quieting reform: Social science and social action in an urban youth program.* Chicago: University of Illinois Press.

Stake, R. E. (1995). *The art of case study research.* Thousand Oaks, CA: Sage.

Stake, R. E., Migotsky, C., Davis, R., Cisneros, E. J., Depaul, G., Dunbar, C., Jr., Farmer, R., Feltovich, J., Johnson, E., Williams, B., Zurita, M., & Chaves, I.

(1997). The evolving synthesis of program value. *Evaluation Practice, 18,* 89-109.

Stronach, I. (1997). Evaluation with the lights out: Deconstructing illuminative evaluation and new paradigm research. In L. Mabry (Ed.), *Evaluation and the postmodern dilemma* (pp. 21-39). Greenwich, CT: JAI.

Stronach, I., & MacLure, M. (1997). *Educational research undone: The postmodern embrace.* Philadelphia: Open University Press.

Taylor, C. (1987). Interpretation and the sciences of man. In P. Rabinow & W. Sullivan (Eds.), *Interpretive social science: A second look* (pp. 33-81). Los Angeles: University of California Press.

Taylor, C. (1995). *Philosophical arguments.* Cambridge MA: Harvard University Press.

Taylor, P. W. (1961). *Normative discourse.* Englewood Cliffs, NJ: Prentice Hall.

Urmson, J. O. (1968). *The emotive theory of ethics.* Oxford: Oxford University Press.

Walzer, M. (1983). *Spheres of justice.* New York: Basic books.

Weiss, C. (1983). Toward the future of stakeholder approaches in evaluation. In A. S. Bryk (Ed.), Stakeholder-based evaluation [Special issue]. *New Directions for Program Evaluation, 17,* 83-96.

Wheelock, A. (1992). *Crossing the tracks.* New York: New Press.

Wittgenstein, L. (1960). *The blue and brown books.* New York: Harper Torchbooks.

Young, I. M. (1990). *Justice and the politics of difference.* Princeton, NJ: Princeton University Press.

AUTHOR INDEX

SUBJECT INDEX

————•◆•————

Ability grouping example, 124-129
Ad hominem model, 83-85
Advocacy, evaluators and, 93, 95-96
American Evaluation Association, ethical standards, 35
Antifoundationalist, 85
Apodictic model, 83
Audiences:
    evaluative reasoning and, 19-21
    stakeholders versus, 20

Bias, 83, 112
Brown v. Board of Education, 49

Cities-in-Schools evaluation, 119
Consensus, 58
Constructions, 62, 58, 7-, 96
Constructivism:
    as social act, 65
    See also Radical constructionist view

Deliberation:
    consideration and, 122-124
    extent of, 122-124
    defined, 101
    democratic, 97. *See also* Deliberative democratic evaluation

evaluative reasoning and, 27-30
reflective, 122
substantive, 27
sufficient, 94
Deliberative democracy, xix-xxi
    views on values, 105
    within political theory, 106-109
    See also Deliberative democratic evaluation
Deliberative democratic evaluation, 91-129
    conclusion, 131-134
    critical questions for, 113-115
    deliberative requirement and, 101-103
    dialogical requirement in, 99-101
    inclusion requirement of, 98-99
    trade-offs in, 126
    values and, 11-14
    See also Deliberative democracy
Democracy:
    deliberative, 97. *See also* Deliberative democratic evaluation
    emotive, 12, 47-54
    participatory, 11
Descriptive valuing, 34, 49, 53
Dialogical interaction, xviii
Dialogical requirement, 99-101
Dialogical view, 55-56

Social programs, needs of disadvan-
    taged and, 50
Social reality, 57, 67
Special interests, 12
"Special pleading" phenomenon, 84-85
Stakeholders:
    audiences versus, 20
    constructions, 96
    deliberation and, 94
    evaluative reasoning and, 19-21
    exclusion of, 117-118
    interests of, 98
    participation of, 59
    representation of, 116-117
Structure of Scientific Revolutions
    (Kuhn), 37
Substantive deliberation, 27

Theoretical perspective, 115
Theory of Justice, A (Rawls), 107
Transgressive validity, 79-81
"Trickle-down" response, 84-85
Truth, 57-58
    positivism and, 63
    regimes of, 76, 78
    seeking, 65
Typology of views, 103-106

U.S. Agency for International Develop-
    ment (USAID), 117
U.S. Defense Department programs, 92
U.S. General Accounting Office, Pro-
    gram Evaluation and Methodology
    Division (PEMD), 91-92
Undecidability of values thesis, 49.
    See also Radical undecidability
    thesis

University of West Indies project, 117

Validity, transgressive, 79
Valuation, meaning of, 5-6
Value assessment, 99
Value claims:
    evaluative reasoning, 15-30
    facts and values, 3-14
    justification of, 68
    See also Values
Value freedom, 35
Value judgments, xv. *See also* Judgments
Value minimalism, xviii, 35, 104
Value-neutrality, 43, 133
Value summaries, 52, 96
"Value-free" doctrine, 4
Values:
    democratic deliberation and, 11-14
    emergent, 9-10
    facts and, 3-14
    meaning of, 5-6
    overarching, 65
    postmodernism and, 75-77
    problem of, xiii-xxi
    radical constructionist view and,
        61-69
    radical undecidability thesis and,
        36-424
    subject to examination, 102
    See also Value claims
Verifiability, positivism and, 37

Welfare-to-work training program, 121

Zeno's paradox, 3-4

ABOUT THE AUTHORS

─────── ·•· ───────

&rnest R. House is Professor in the School of Education at the University of Colorado at Boulder. Previously, he was at the Center for Instructional Research and Curriculum Evaluation (CIRCE) at the University of Illinois in Urbana-Champaign. He has been a visiting scholar at the University of California, Los Angeles, Harvard University, and the University of New Mexico, as well as at universities in England, Australia, Spain, Sweden, Austria, and Chile. His primary research interests are in the areas of educational evaluation and policy analysis. His books include *The Politics of Educational Innovation* (1974), *Survival in the Classroom* (with S. Lapan, 1978), *Evaluating With Validity* (1980), *Jesse Jackson and the Politics of Charisma* (1988), *Professional Evaluation: Social Impact and Political Consequences* (1993), and *Schools for Sale* (1998). He is the 1989 recipient (with W. Madura) of the Harold E. Lasswell Prize in policy sciences and the 1990 recipient of the Paul F. Lazarsfeld Award for Evaluation Theory, presented by the American Evaluation Association. He has served as editor (with R. Wooldridge) of *New Directions in Program Evaluation* (1982-1985) and as a featured columnist for *Evaluation Practice* (1984-1989). He is a Senior Fellow at the Center for Advanced Study in the Behavioral Sciences at Stanford, 1999-2000.

$\mathcal{K}$enneth R. Howe is Professor in the School of Education, University of Colorado at Boulder, specializing in educational ethics and philosophy of education. He has published more than 40 articles and chapters on a variety of topics, ranging from the quantitative/qualitative debate in educational research to a philosophical defense of multicultural education. He has published two previous books: *The Ethics of Special Education* (with Ofelia Miramontes) and *Understanding Equal Educational Opportunity: Social Justice, Democracy and Schooling.* He teaches courses in the Teacher Certification Program and the Graduate Program in Educational Foundations, Policy, and Practice at Boulder.